THE MAN OF GOD WALKS ALONE

OREST STOCCO

THE MAN OF GOD WALKS ALONE

ISBN 978-1-926442-10-5

Edited by Penny Lynn Cates
Cover Design by Penny Lynn Cates

More Talks with St. Padre Pio
Volume 2

"Life is a flight of the alone to the Alone."

Plotinus

A Note from the Author

On Monday, August 9, 2010 I went for my first session with a gifted psychic medium who channeled the Roman Catholic Saint Padre Pio. This was the first of ten monthly sessions that became the basis of my novel *Healing with Padre Pio,* and each session gradually shifted my attitude from one of vanity to humility.

I would probably have gone to my grave oblivious to the depths of my spiritual conceit had I not been blessed with St. Padre Pio's love and understanding, for which I will always be grateful; and after I wrote *Healing with Padre Pio* I wanted to continue my relationship with him, so I wrote him personal letters.

After I published two volumes of letters to Padre Pio, I decided to talk to him directly like my psychic medium, but not quite in the same way. Since I'm not a psychic, I could neither see nor hear St. Padre Pio; but by practicing a technique that Carl Jung called "active imagination," I spoke with St. Padre Pio in the same way that Neale Donald Walsch spoke with God in *Conversations with God* and other books.

"Active imagination" is a dialogue with the unconscious; a dialectical exercise in reconciling the unconscious with the conscious self. A novelist, for example, engages his unconscious to produce the images that he needs to reconcile elements of his unconscious with his conscious self; just as Neale Donald Walsch did with his conversations with God. He engaged his unconscious to resolve personal issues, and his unconscious spoke to him by way of an archetypal God image. In like manner, I spoke with the archetypal image of St. Padre Pio in my first book of dialogues *In the Shade of the Maple Tree* and resolved many of my personal issues.

The question of whether Neale Donald Walsch actually spoke with God or not is left open, because there is no way he could prove that it was God he spoke with, just as I cannot prove that my dialogues with St. Padre Pio were with the departed spirit of the Capuchin monk who suffered the stigmata for fifty years; but just as Neale Donald Walsch's conversations with God were real enough for him, my talks with St. Padre Pio were real enough for me; and I continued.

Whether it was St. Padre Pio or my creative unconscious, or in some mystical way both, I enjoyed my active imagination experience. Not only did our dialogues help to relieve me of many of life's anxieties, but they opened up perspectives I would not have been aware of, and for this I am grateful; and with his permission I'm only too happy to share our new dialogues with you.

Orest Stocco
Georgian Bay, Ontario
June 11, 2015

Table of Contents

1. If I May, Padre...

Thursday, November 13, 2014

"Penny and I felt like watching a movie last week, but it was too late to go out; so I went online to see what we could watch, and when I came across Shirley MacLaine's *Out on a Limb* I was strongly nudged to watch it again. I have most of her books, my favorite being *Saging While Aging*; but I wanted Penny to enjoy Shirley MacLaine's spiritual journey, which for all intents and purposes began with her book *Out on a Limb*. She financed, produced, and starred in the movie version of her book, and the following night we watched part two. We loved both parts, and the next day I took out her book *I'm Over All That* and read it again, and then I dug up *The Camino* and read that again also, wondering why she didn't make a movie of that book. Would that have been too much for the viewer? It got pretty heavy when she went into her past lives with John the Scot and Atlantis and Lemuria and her androgynous lifetime. That spooked a lot of readers, and I'm sure she was advised to not pursue that possibility. Nonetheless, I'm very glad she wrote *The Camino*. It parted the veil to the spiritual side of life a lot more because of her very high public profile. Journalists hounded her when they found out she was doing the age-old pilgrimage along the Santiago de Compostela Camino in Spain. After I read *The Camino* I read Paulo Coelho's *The Pilgrimage* again, which is the account of his own trek on the Santiago de Compostela Camino; but it wasn't as exciting as Shirley MacLaine's spiritual journey, because she awakened to her past lives that spoke to the profound mysteries of life and the Way. As much as I like Coelho's books (*The Alchemist* has sold over sixty million copies), something about him bothers me; I think because of his personal history with magic which left its mark on him, but I can get into that another time. I just wanted to open up another dialogue with you because I brought my first book of dialogues with you to closure but would like to continue our talks. If I may, Padre; are you up to another dialogue with me?"

"I would love another dialogue. The more you stretch your creative muscles, the better it is for both of us."

"I know it would be good for me, but how would it be good for you?"

"Didn't Shirley MacLaine say to Oprah Winfrey on her show that we are all one? That all seekers were her and she was all seekers?"

"Yes, she did. When Oprah asked her if she was responsible for ushering in the New Age movement. Shirley very modestly deflected that question by saying that she found herself on a path that she had to explore. I thought her answer was brilliant. It showed how much she had been humbled by her own quest for self."

"Exactly. And that's what it's all about. As I said in one of our talks for your novel Healing with Padre Pio, life is a journey of the self; and Shirley MacLaine is on her journey and you are on yours, as is every person—"

"If I may interrupt here, I'd like to ask you a question that's been bothering me ever since I became aware of it. When Shirley answered Oprah by saying that we are all one and Oprah rephrased her question to get Shirley to admit her part in ushering in the New Age, I saw a paradox in Shirley's answer; and my question is this: if we are all one, what does this say for the journey of the self?"

"Aye, there's the rub as Shakespeare would say! That's very perceptive of you. But that's only because you have coincided with your true self and have realized the distinction between the all in One and the One in all. The journey of the self is becoming the One in all; and not until one coincides with the One will one realize his true self. This is what life is all about."

"May I continue this dialogue later? I have some things to attend to, prepare dinner and then go out and rake the rest of the leaves before the snow flies, which could be this weekend. Besides, I need my best energies to talk about this mysterious journey of the self. There's much more to it than meets the eye."

"I agree. Yes, by all means; tend to your chores…"

Next morning…

"I put on a pot of pasta sauce and meatballs for dinner (I will use the left-over sauce today for eggplant parmigiana) and then went out to rake leaves. I raked all the leaves that had blown into the ditch line of our front lawn and packed them into our large garbage container, but I didn't' dump them in the empty lot where we dump all our leaves; I went back inside to check on the sauce and never went out again. I wanted to go out and finish raking, but I felt too winded (God, how I despair my physical condition since my heart operation!), and last night it snowed; so I have to wait and see if the snow melts to rake the rest of the leaves. Otherwise it won't be until the spring. Now, back to the journey of the self.

"This was my problem with the Buddhist teaching, which states that we are all one Self and with which I don't disagree; but to realize we are all one Self is what the journey of the self is all about. In other words, we cannot dismiss the evolutionary process of life by stating that the end product is the same as the beginning; because if that is the case then what would be the point of evolution? The acorn seed is not an oak tree until it grows into an oak tree; in like manner, we have to grow in consciousness (in spirit, if you will) to become our true Self. Isn't this what you and I agreed upon in my novel *Healing with Padre Pio*?"

"Yes. This is the distinction. As you say, what would be the point of evolution if not to grow and evolve in consciousness? If I may be allowed to say this, do not despair about your heart condition. It is what it is and it is your new normal. Learn to adjust your life in your new condition, which can be improved upon if you took time each day to exercise; but you know that already, so I need not remind you. It is your responsibility. Now, back to the concept of going out on a limb, which Shirley MacLaine certainly did with her private life and you are doing with yours. But she had such a public profile that she risked her career by going out, and she deserves a lot of credit for parting the veil on man's spiritual life by telling the world about reincarnation and UFOs. That took enormous courage."

"That's why I have always championed her whenever someone called her a kook. I'm amazed at the arrogance of some people's ignorance, how they can be so judgmental when they know so little."

3

"It's fear of the unknown that makes people defensive. Whenever someone's belief system is threatened by the unknown the fight or flight instinct kicks in, and they react; some defending their beliefs by denying the unknown, and some dismissing the unknown as total nonsense, as many have done with Shirley MacLaine. But she stuck to her beliefs despite all the ridicule and has given many people license to explore their own lives. She was a trailblazer, even though she likes to play this down as she did with Oprah."

"Padre, if you don't mind; I'd like to veer off in another direction. I've not been the same since we came back from up north where we tended to our triplex which we put up for sale. I see now that we have to install an interconnected fire alarm system, which has given me new cause for worry. Why do I worry so much? Your constant refrain when you were on earth was, 'pray, hope, and don't worry.' I'm sure that over the years that you heard confessions you heard the worries of all your penitents, which must have opened your heart to man's troubled soul; but what is the cause of this insidious fear?"

"You're right to call it fear, because that's what it is. It is the fear of separation from the security of our own mind. We have images of our own comfortable world where life cannot harm us, but life has its own course that it must follow, and learning how to stay in sync with life is the key to solving the problem of constant worrying. We worry because we fear change. But change is necessary to stay in sync with life. This is the biggest challenge man has, forever staying abreast of life. But life is always changing, and today it is changing very quickly because of the digital revolution. Make up your mind to stay abreast and do your best. I will be with you every step of the way. All will be okay. I promise."

"I was hoping you would say that. I feel so insecure now that I think I may have to install an interconnecting fire alarm system in our triplex to have it up to code so we can sell it. What a hassle. But if it has to be done, I'd like you to walk me through it so that I don't suffer from excessive anxiety. It's not good for my heart. I felt it yesterday when I got the news, and I had to calm down. I don't know how much more I can stand the pressures of life, but I don't like it because it's affecting my writing. I've lost the stamina for writing. I begin something and can't seem to finish it. I've still got a spiritual musing to finish, and I can't seem to get into anything new. I don't know what to do, Padre."

"Consolidate your energies. Concentrate on one thing and do it. And don't watch so much TV. It's dissipating your energies. Force yourself to read if you have to, because reading focuses the mind and concentrates your energies. Even quiet time contemplating is better than watching too much television. I know TV can be very informative, but then it becomes an excuse to sit and do nothing. That's the habit you have to break. Doing nothing but watching TV keeps you from DOING, and DOING is your key to a happier life. DO and you will BE the person you want to be, a writer full of ideas bursting to come out. I promise you!"

"I suppose if I'm not up to reading or writing I could edit one of my manuscripts. I can't help but feel that my manuscript *Cathedral of my Past Lives* is ready to take out. I can hear it calling to me. It's faint, but it is calling to me. I do hope I get this book out before I cross over to the other side. But let's not go there now; suffice to say that I have to get off my ass and start DOING. So, if you will pardon me; I'm going to shower and wash my hair, and then I'm going to get dinner ready while Penny's still at work, and then I'm going to go for a walk and think about which manuscript I should work on—maybe my novel *The Waking Dream,* which features my incredible dream with C. G. Jung. I can hear you, and I know I should finish my book of short stories (*Enantiodromia and Other Stories*); but I'm not quite sure what to do with that book yet. I'm still too afraid to finish it. Maybe if you gave me a good kick in the butt I might get to it; but that's not your way, is it Padre? Anyway, until we talk again—"

"Ciao for now, my friend..."

2. My Prayer from God

Wednesday, November, 19, 2014

"Can we talk, Padre?"

"Yes, by all means. Don't' think about what it is you want to say; just let your heart speak for you."

"My heart is aching. I am suffering from an overwhelming sense of fear. I know it's a false fear, but it came out of nowhere yesterday with the weather, believe it or not. The snow storm that swept through the province dropped a lot of snow on my hometown of Nipigon and we had a problem finding someone to plow the two driveways of our triplex, and then we found out the fridge went out on the top apartment unit and we had to look into it, and Penny went to work here in Georgian Bay with white-out conditions and this scared the hell out of me; thank God she came home safe. I wanted to drink a whole bottle of brandy last night and just phase out, but I didn't. That's why I want to talk with you today. I tried to read yesterday to pass the time, and I finished writing a private letter to a friend who has cancer, but I couldn't bring myself to send it to her, and I don't think I will. It may become part of a short story someday. I finished reading a book on C. G. Jung (*Jung Stripped Bare*, by Sonu Shamdasani), but it didn't do what I hoped it would and lift me up to a higher place, and I watched TV and all the junk and negative imagery heightened my anxiety and I just didn't know what to do. Thank God Penny made it home safe. I poured us a couple of glasses of wine before dinner and I felt safer with Penny home. Padre, what's happening to me? I was ready to leave this life—"

"It was a tumultuous day for many people yesterday all across the province because of the weather. The weather has a way of stirring up emotions. It has begun to settle down, so today will be a lot better."

"I hope so. But I cannot get over the feeling of my insignificance. I feel like my life has been turned into a perspective that has reduced me to a mere speck in the vast cosmic scheme of things, and my insignificance weighs upon me. It's like all the searching that I have done—and I was a pathological seeker!—has added up to a big fat zero. What am I, anyway? Just another drop in the bucket of life!"

"Aren't we all? Life is a grand gesture of God, and merely to be a drop in the gesture of God is no mean thing. We are all souls, and we all are a part of God; and in our own insignificant way we are as relevant to God as the whole bucket. This is the mystery of the Divine. You had a bad day yesterday, that's all."

"I wish I could buy into that, but it goes beyond that for me. It's not just the day; it's my life. The winged chariot is drawing near and I have not seen my dream come true. I'm still waiting, and I am tired. I am tired of life, Padre. Last night as I lay on the couch trying to divert myself with TV I thought of just how difficult life really is and wondered why souls feel privileged to come to earth to grow. Life is very difficult, and it doesn't get any easier. It just changes, but the difficulties are always there; and after a while one gets so fatigued one wants to leave this place called life. I took a sleeping pill last night just so I could go into that state of consciousness where I can get away from it all. Do you know that I came out of my open heart surgery with the comment, "That was the best sleep I had in my life"? If that doesn't tell you something, nothing will—"

"Yes, it was revealing. You were sleep deprived; but I know what you are talking about. You need to express yourself. You need to transcend this state of worry consciousness. You need to lift yourself above yourself. And the way to do that is to go on a diet—a bad news diet. Stop listening to the news for a week or two, and don't watch so much TV. Keep yourself busy writing and reading. That's the only way you can lift yourself above the worry belt, if I may use that phrase."

"I have a question I'd like to ask. Do negative thoughts activate what can be called "the Trickster"? It just seems that when I'm caught in a negative zone the Trickster has a way of adding to my anxiety. Can you explain that, please?"

"I know what you mean. In my day we called the Trickster the Devil; but it is all about energy. We attract Trickster energy when we are in a negative zone. This is pretty much the way it goes. At least you recognize it. Most people don't. I didn't when I was on earth. I felt like I was under constant attack by the Devil, but it was the nature

of my vocation that activated the Trickster, as you put it. But because you are conscious of it, you have, as you like to say, caught the Devil by the tail."

"And what would be the best way to keep the Trickster at bay?"

"As I said, lift yourself up above the worry belt. From the moment you feel the dark cloud moving in, stop and shift your attention to all the good in your life—your loves and accomplishments, and start your gratitude prayer. The gratitude prayer is one of the best ways to drive the dark clouds away. I promise you!"

"If I may, I'd like to know if I am doing the right thing by not sending my friend the letter I wrote her. I feel it might be too much. Advice, please?"

"Listen to your heart. You wrote your letter in good faith, thinking that it may help her in her desperate hour; but second thoughts prevent you from sending it. I would sit on it for a while longer. You will know what to do in a day or so."

"Am I being exploitive by thinking it would make a great story? Have I become a whore for my writing?"

"Life is what it is. You don't create life, as such; you live it. A writer writes about life. Strictly speaking, no you are not being exploitive; but if you have qualms about writing a story about the people you know perhaps you shouldn't be writing. It's that simple. When people came to confession, I didn't question their existence; I listened to their sins and all their woes and blessed them in the name of God; in my blessing I did what I was supposed to do. Writing stories is your blessing. It is what you are supposed to do. You are not responsible for the way people live their lives just as I was not responsible for the sins committed that the people who came to me to confess; we are responsible for our own lives, and all we can do is what we are called to do—me to absolve and bless the people who came to me, and you to write about the people who come into your life. Don't feel bad about the personal nature of your writing. If it wasn't for the personal nature, where would literature be? The best literature is the most personal. This is where we learn about life. As I said, you bless the world with your writing. It is your prayer to God."

"What a wonderful spin you put on it—"

"Don't be sarcastic. It is not a spin. I am telling you what you need to hear. You have come too far to be so cynical. It's not a bad thing to be cynical, but when you let it get the better of you it becomes a cancer that will consume you. There are a lot of people that are overcome with cynicism, which only exacerbates the problem; but you are not one of them. You have worked too hard to find your way, and it is your duty to live your life in the light of God's love. Dwell on the positive, and let gratitude be your daily prayer; and write your stories. This is how you will lift yourself above the worry belt and stop feeling sorry for yourself. I promise all will be well. Just be grateful for what you have and the dark cloud will part and the light will shine back into your life. JUST DO!"

"I hear you….I went out and DID the driveway; or, one half of it so Penny can get the car out when she goes to work, and I will do the other half later after I'm rested up. I don't want to worry Penny. She doesn't want me to shovel snow at all for fear of a heart attack; but I have to do something to keep busy. Anyway, DOING is the key to lifting myself above the worry belt. And as I shoveled the driveway I did my gratitude prayer, thanking Divine Spirit for the first love in my life (Penny, of course), and all the other things that I'm grateful for; so thank you, Padre. Your advice works—when I take it!"

"You're welcome, my friend."

"I'm going to break off now to do some reading. I've decided to read some of Glenda Green's book *Love without End, Jesus Speaks*. I've read it several times already, but it's such a good story I want to read it again just for the high energy that it gives me. So, until we talk again…"

9

3. And So It Goes

Friday, November 21, 2014

"I have to talk with you. I've just heard from Penny who called from the Canadian Tire Service Department and got a shock. She had an appointment to put on new tires for the car and learned that it needs a lot of work, more than three thousand dollars of work on the brakes and corroded fuel line and other things which I'm not sure of because I went into shock when Penny told me that the mechanic told her that given the mileage of our little Honda Civic it would be wiser to trade it in for a new car rather than invest that kind of money on repairs; so there you have it, Padre. I was going to go for a walk, but it's snowing out; so I decided to exercise my active imagination and talk with you instead. What to do?"

"Life does surprise us every now and then, but please don't take this to heart; after all, your car does have a lot of mileage and service was expected. Ponder your decision with your loved one and decide together."

"I guess what bothers me is that investing in a new car will draw upon the money Penny inherited from her father's estate this past summer, and that will cut into the little security that we had; but if it has to be done, it has to be done. I do think we have to get a new car, but we weren't expecting to do so until next summer. I guess the schedule got moved up, that's all. God, I don't know what to say."

"Everything will work out for the best, I promise you. It takes a little courage to jump into the fray, but once in life unfolds accordingly; and your life is on track now, so don't fuss about what you have no control over. Some decisions in life have to be made, because not making them only prolongs the agony; so make your decision and let God take care of the rest. It will be okay. Trust me."

"I needed to hear that, even if it's only coming from my need to be consoled; but that shouldn't matter, should it?"

"Not at all. Love is who we are, and from Love comes love; so don't fret about what is, because Love is all there is. Open your heart

and put your trust in God. It is much easier than you think. Sit back and let your heart open. I will wait."

"Okay. Thank you, Padre…"

4. And So It Went

"Saturday we drove into Midland Honda and bought a new 2014 Honda Civic, which went a lot smoother than I expected. We traded in our old Honda, and because we still had fifteen hundred dollars owing on it (to Honda, who financed the car) we got a zero percent rate on the new financing; so our payments for our new car are three hundred a month, which Penny thinks we can manage. We should be getting the car this week, or next; they have to bring it in from another dealer. It's blue, like our old car. We could have gotten it in grey, or white; but Penny gave me the choice, and I chose blue. Everything went okay; better than okay, actually. It just felt like everything fell into place, starting with the young lady who sold us the car. She had a wonderful coincidence story to share with us (how she met her second husband), and I shared my incredible coincidence story of how we got the lot for our new house here in Georgian Bay, and the sale of our car just moved along like it was meant to be; so, thank you Padre."

"A new car equals new mobility, literally and metaphorically; and I am happy for you. Your path is widening, your life will unfold blessedly; and all you have to do is concentrate on your writing. You have too many things started and not enough focus; so FOCUS on one work and tap into the Source."

"I know. I've been doing everything to keep from writing, justifying myself by exploring the lives and works of successful people—like the actor Frank Langella and Shirley MacLaine, and yesterday I went back to Caroline Myss whose book I'm still reading (*Entering the Castle*); I watched three of her most recent talks on You Tube yesterday, and she still impresses me with her spiritual wisdom. If I may, I'd like to ask you if she's being guided in her talks by St. Teresa of Avila, as I suspect."

"Yes, just as I am guiding you in your daily life. She has a very good relationship with St. Teresa; special, in fact, because

Caroline was chosen to get the Word out to the world. She's quite the ambassador for the new teaching."

"The new teaching? Pray tell, what new teaching?"

"Caroline likes to call it hard ball spirituality, which it is; but it's the teaching the world needs today. It's basically the same age-old teaching of spiritual growth through individual effort, but dressed up to suit the modern world, which Caroline does very well. And you also. This is what you are doing with your writing, despite what you may think. You don't want to call yourself a teacher, but your writing is all about the new teaching. It can't help but be so, because you have transcended the old paradigms and speak from a new perspective. In many ways, you and Caroline are the same; and it wouldn't hurt to send her some of your books. She might just be of service to you. Give it a shot. Trust me."

"She called you 'the Great Pio' yesterday in her talk, which made me smile because it reflects what the world (those who know about you, that is) thinks of you, and which I can confirm given the experience of writing *Healing with Padre Pio*. But you don't come through to me the way St. Teresa comes through to Caroline; why is that? Is Caroline more intuitive? She definitely is, because she's been a medical intuitive most of her life. Is that it? And speaking of intuition, I love what she had to say about it. It's not a gift; it's a natural instinct, and the only way to develop it is by growing spiritually—which to her meant an ethical life. Which is the same conclusion that I came to long ago. The more we grow spiritually, the more blessed we are with the gift of sight; right?"

"Absolutely. But to answer your question, she does have a very special relationship with St. Teresa because of their mutual Sacred Contract. We have a Sacred Contract also, but slightly different; and in due time all will come to pass as it should. It's all a matter of readiness. Each step brings you closer to the center of your being, and once you step into the core of your soul you will shine like no other, for such is the light of your life. Again, I must tell you to trust me."

"I will. Can you tell me what you think of the new little book I finally got started—*The Pearl of Great Price*? I've been nudged to write this book, but I think what got me started was the dream that my friend with cancer had. She dreamt of receiving a pearl and a coin, which to me spoke of Christ's parable of the pearl of great price; and I would like to end my little book with her dream, because it would prove the profound significance of Christ's parable. What do you think?"

"It is a very real story with a very real ending, and Christ's parable is the theme that holds it all together. Please give this book your best energy. It is going to be a special book with a special meaning. Don't fight the energy of this book. You have outlined the chapter titles as they came to you; trust the creative spirit to take you where your story needs to go. Of all your books, this is the one you have to trust the most. Just let the chapters find their own way to the Source."

"With your blessing then, I'm going to give it my best shot. I've been nudged to re-read Paulo Coelho's book *The Pilgrimage* as background material for this book, as well as Glenda Green's *Love without End*; and, I have to tell you that I've also been nudged to re-read the New Testament again to re-acquaint myself with the teaching that Jesus gave to the world—the secret teaching, that is."

"Excellent. And while you're at it, re-read Ecclesiastes. It will inform that part of your book that needs to be informed."

"Okay, one more thing before I sign off. I've also been inspired to read St. Teresa of Avila's book *The Way of Perfection*, which means that I will have to read her book *Interior Castle* as well, and perhaps St. John's *Dark Night of the Soul*. Do I have to read these books as I write *The Pearl of Great Price*?

"They will go a long way in helping you with the request you were going to ask me; so, yes, by all means read them."

"Thank you for sparing me having to spell out my request. I'm too ashamed to talk about it openly; but if I had to, I would."

"I know. But you have nothing to be ashamed of. Your life is fraught with the creative life force, and when it is not given adequate expression it must find a way to release the pressure on your psyche. So don't worry about it. It's one and the same energy, regardless how it expresses itself. But when it is expressed creatively, such as in your writing, it will serve a larger purpose; and that elevates your life and takes you to new horizons of spiritual growth. So FOCUS on your writing and let the juices flow freely into your stories. That's your blessing, and calling."

"Fair enough. Until we talk again, then…"

5. Abandoned of Purpose

Monday, December 8, 2014

"Padre, I feel like I have been dumped on by a ton of insignificance, and I don't know what to do about it. I've not been the same since we came back from up north; my life seems to have taken a different feel. I don't know what this feel is. It's like I have been abandoned of purpose. I told Penny that the other day and she said, "Oh, no; don't go into a funk." But it's not a funk. I just feel—not lost, but not found either; and that's a very strange feel. I haven't "dialogued" with you for a while, trying my hardest to write other stuff—I did start *The Pearl of Great Price*, and I did write a new spiritual musing ("The Full but Incomplete Life"), but I'm not really happy in my writing these days. I feel like it's all a pouring into the void. There's no reception for my writing. Even my blog is not getting many views. What's with that, Padre? Can you shed some light on my life? I feel desperate, but not desperate. I am too worn out to feel desperate, and I am even too tired to be afraid; but I am. Deep down inside I still harbor fear. Last night I dreamt of yellow roses on the side of a mountain that I had to climb, and on the ground strawberries grew; and I felt good because the roses and strawberries augured good fortune. What's that all about?"

"You're going through a change of consciousness. Your trip up north was the catalyst that precipitated your change of consciousness, and now you are experiencing life differently. It's not a bad thing. It's a way of living that allows you to see the ephemerality of life. But life is not ephemeral, as such; it's the process that soul needs to realize itself. You know this, and you write about this in your own way; and your writing is not irrelevant; it has a power all of its own which will find its readers in the course of time—"

"Yeah, right; here we go again. When will you stop singing that song? It doesn't comfort me anymore. It's taking too long, and that horse has died!"

"When all is said and done, you know that this life is all about the individual soul working its way back home to God; so what does it matter if you get acknowledged the way you want to or not as long as you succeed in your journey? It's not about them; it's all about the individual soul. That's the point of it all."

"And the object of the lesson is to learn to help other souls find their way to God, is that it?"

"Service to life is what it all comes down to in the end."

"But it's all so fatiguing. I read the papers and watch TV and it's all so fatiguing, like the world doesn't know what it's all about, and people go on their merry way asleep to the whole purpose of their existence. People don't want to know why they were born and meant to do; all they want is to get the most out of life, or avenge their wounded pride, or boast their accomplishments. It's all so silly!"

"From your perspective now it is, but as you step out of this point of view life will take on a new meaning; and you will bound with purpose. I promise you!"

"I can't wait! Now, where did my creative energy go? What do I have to do to get it back? Please tell me, because I feel abandoned of purpose—"

"Write, write, and write some more. All you have to do is write to connect with your purpose. It's as simple as that, I promise you."

"I can't seem to focus like I used to. I feel like I've lost the sense of the moment, that NOW of my life. That's why I feel abandoned of purpose."

"Purpose is direction. Writing is seeking direction. The more you write, the more direction you will have. Write your way back to purpose. That's the magic formula you are looking for. Don't expect anything more, and the world will come to you in your realized purpose. Your writing is your way, your pay, your salvation, and your happiness. It is what you've always wanted, so do it."

"Don't you get tired of lecturing me?"

"No. It's my joy to work with you. You have no idea how wonderful it is to help another soul work its way out of its conundrums. It's as rewarding for me as it is for you when you liberate yourself from your limitations. That's what service to life is all about and why I love working with you."

"Is it work, really? I'm not too fond of that. I'd rather like to see our relationship as one of—well, just friendship of a special kind."

"I understand, and I agree with you; and so it shall be, my friend."

"Padre, I'm going to make a request of a special kind. I would like to get a taste of the divine, the spiritual life, other realities—to see you in my dreams, if you will, and experiences of that nature. Why can't this be so?"

"It can. All you have to do is ask."

"I just did."

"And it shall be so. Let yourself go into the experience and the door will open to other realities that you long to be a part of your life. I know you are bored with your dreams, but you are working off some of your parallel life karma in your dreams; but the time has come to shift gears. So, let go and let God."

"Okay, I will. Thank you."

"You're welcome. Now, try to focus on your writing, please."

"Will do…."

6. Doing Some Shadow Work

Friday, December 19, 2014

"Padre, it's been a while since our last talk and the idea occurred to me this morning to employ this exercise in active imagination to do some shadow work. This is a Jungian concept, and it entails a confrontation with one's shadow for the purpose of expanding one's self-consciousness. In effect, it's a conscious way of processing the dark, repressed side of one's personality and integrating it with one's conscious personality. Are you game?"

"This may prove more interesting than you think. After all, you are going to be delving into some corners of your psyche that you have not yet explored, and you may find stuff there that may disturb you; but I will be there to guide you, as Virgil guided Dante."

"Let's begin, then. I still have issues with my ego needs for acknowledgement. I want to go deep into myself and explore the origin of this need. I know that ego can never really be satisfied, because it's to the nature of ego consciousness to never be satisfied, it being a consciousness of being and becoming—the very heart and soul of the individuation process; but, still, I have this need to be acknowledged for the writer that I have become. For example, this morning I posted a spiritual musing called "Kitchen Angel" on my Spiritual Musings Blog, and then I shared it on Twitter, Facebook, and Spiritual Networks; but I only picked up six viewers from the States, none from Canada yet, nor anywhere else. What's going on?"

"The day's not over yet. You have to remember, you have a history with your spiritual musings that demands thought from your viewers; and not to put too fine a point on it, most viewers don't want to think too deeply. You threaten your viewers with your blog. They don't want to do serious thinking. That's why you don't get the kind of acknowledgment that you seek. It will come in time, when your books take off, as the saying goes. Patience. That's the virtue you must practice."

"That's a fair explanation; but it doesn't satisfy me, really. I still feel like there's something more, something that I'm not getting."

"There's always something more. You can dig as deep as you like, and there will always be another level. This is the nature of the psyche."

"Can you tell me then what it is that I'm not getting? Then perhaps we can dig a little deeper into the origins of my insecurity."

"What you're not getting is that your life is an individual journey and has nothing to do with another soul's journey. Every soul is on its own path to God, and what that soul does is that soul's relationship with itself, and God. Your relationship with yourself and God is yours alone, and to expect others to acknowledge how you relate to yourself and God is asking an awful lot of them. People couldn't be bothered about other people's relationship with themselves and God; all they want to know is about the private goings-on, all of that juicy private stuff that confirms their own misery. But you don't feed into that. Your life is all about trying to resolve the misery; that's why your musings are too thoughtful. But I will see what I can do to get more viewers to your blog. I happen to like your musings. They cut to the chase, and people need to hear this. It's good for their soul."

"I'd appreciate it also if they got to check on my books while they're on my blog. And speaking of books, I'm not sure if I told you this but I did start writing *The Pearl of Great Price.* I think I did, but I've been off it this past while. I've been working on my spiritual musings. I've gotten a few more titles for musings, and I'm kind of anxious to see what comes of them. This morning I got the title "Pursing the Unhypocritical Life," which I'd like to explore. I think you'd like that, because if I'm not mistaken I quote what you said about hypocrisy; but that's a very delicate subject, because people don't want to be seen for what they are. Wouldn't you agree? Given the hypocrisy that you had to witness in your life, I'm sure you'd like to see what my Muse has to say about it."

"Hypocrisy is a delicate subject, as you say; and yet, this is the way of the world. It always was, and it always will be; and the most that we can do about it is to put our thoughts out there for those that need them. Do your best. I look forward to seeing how your creative gift works out this theme. You do have a way of putting things

together that adds a measure of clarity to a subject. With my blessing, work out your musing on hypocrisy. I'll do what I can to help you along."

"I'm going into Midland to get my papers and some grocery items for Penny, but I'll be closing now with some regret because I still feel like I'm a thousand miles from where I'd like to be; and I don't know what I can do about it. The thought came to me to look up Oprah Winfrey's address and send her some of my books to see if this could get the ball rolling. What do you think?"

"Do what you feel you should. Nothing happens by chance. Every action is precipitated by an action, so get your books out there and see what chain of events it may engender. Not only Oprah. Try some others as well. With my blessings."

"Thank you. Until the next time…"

7. Was that You?

Sunday, December 21, 2014

"Was that you? On my drive to Midland yesterday, the idea just came to me to write a new book of essays on the shadow and shadow work. The title of my book came to me out of the blue (from you, I suspect)—*Shadow Work, Essays on the Art of Conscious Self-Actualization.* And I was even given the title of the first essay, "A Necessary Presumption," the theme being on why I am qualified to write about the shadow and shadow work because of my own "confrontation with the unconscious," to use Jung's phrase. This idea excites me, but I'm not sure I should tackle it given that I've started writing *The Pearl of Great Price.* I know I can do both, and they would probably work with each other; what do you think?"

"If you feel you can take on the job, go for it; and don't try to puzzle out where the idea came from. Your creative Muse is your inspiration, which in the final analysis is Divine Spirit—"

"No. I refuse to accept that answer. That's a deflection that I'm only too familiar with. The mind can be pretty tricky, and I'd like some independent thought on the issue. Either you inspired me or you didn't. Which is it?"

"It was me. I'd like to see you explore the subject of the shadow and shadow work through the creative process and not through talks with me as you had originally planned. What comes out of our talks will assist you, but the creative essay is your forte. You have a talent for dialectical thinking, and you can scour the depths of the soul with your creative reasoning. Get your book started and see where it takes you. You will know by the end of your first essay whether it is worth continuing or not, because you know very well if your Muse wants you to continue you will be given clues along the way, as always happens with all your books."

"Alright, I'll try writing the first essay; maybe today."

"Good. Now go about your day and let it unfold gracefully."

"Until we talk again…

8. The Phone Call

Tuesday, December 23, 2014

"I got a phone call last night from Eddie, our friend Alice's son, and he didn't have good news. His mother was in the hospital, in the palliative care ward, and expected to die in a few days. Eddie's mother asked him to call me, and when Eddie informed me of his mother's sudden turn I broke into tears. I knew that if she lasted the winter it would be a miracle, so I shouldn't have been surprised by the phone call; but the sudden shock still threw me, and I broke down when Eddie put his mother on the phone. I couldn't control my emotions, Padre; and I felt foolish after because I may have said things I shouldn't have. But they just came out of my mouth. I wanted her to know that she had made the right decision for her healing journey— going the holistic way instead of having surgery for her tumor; because I didn't want her going to the other side feeling like she had made the wrong decision. Penny and I are going to Orillia today to visit her, hoping she's still with us; and perhaps I can be a little more contained in my emotions. I don't know what to say to her, and I'd like you to be there with me. I need your steady surety. Would you, please?"

"Yes, of course. Your emotions were spontaneous, because of your great love for her. She appreciated being told that she had made the right decision. Do not beat yourself up over nothing. You said what had to be said for her to have peace of mind. I will be with you today, and what will happen will happen. It's in God's hands."

"She called your name out from a dream one night last summer, and she was prompted to visit me. She was reading my novel *Healing with Padre Pio*, and I guess you must have been with her on the inner planes; were you?"

"Yes. She needed the information that your book had to offer, and once she made the connection with her own vanity, she had to talk with you. Your book had a great influence on her thinking, and

she's still in wonder of you. When you visit, be yourself. Don't try to be contained in your emotions. Let your heart speak. It is the best when you are yourself. I promise you, it will be okay."

"I don't have much of a choice, do I? I always fall back on my instinctive self when life crowds me into a corner, and I expect I will do the same today when we visit; but I wish I could be a little more self-contained. I'll do the best I can. I know now that I will have to finish writing *The Pearl of Great Price* this winter, because Alice's story is central to the theme—which is the quest for my true self, and what Alice's journey was all about. She got the pearl of great price in her dream, which completes my story aesthetically; and I know I have to tell it."

"It is central to your story, not only because it compliments your story but because it adds a dimension of greater credibility. Knowing that it happened to another person will strengthen the theme of your story, especially in how your friend pursued her own path in her own way. This is what the journey of the self is all about; not walking in another's footsteps, but walking one's own path."

"Padre, do you mind if I do a little active imagination on what I might say at my friend's service, or would this be too much?"

"Now is not the time. When she has crossed over you may be allowed to practice active imagination. It goes against the spiritual grain to practice active imagination with people still alive. It is an interference in their psychic space."

"I gathered as much. Thank you for confirming that."

"You're welcome"

"On to another subject. Penny went to the mailbox after work last night and came home with her Christmas gift for me—eight new books for me to read over the Christmas holidays and the rest of this winter. I'm going to list them here, and then I want to ask you something. They are: *The Freud/Jung Letters*; *Atom and Archetype, The Pauli/Jung Letters*; *The Boy Who Died and Came Back*, by Robert Moss; *Joan Grant, Speaking from the Heart: Ethics, Reincarnation, & What It Means to Be Human*; *The Heart's Code*, by Paul Pearsall, Ph. D; *You Can't Go Home Again*, by Thomas Wolfe; and a biography, *Updike*, by Adam Begley. You can see that I'm going to have some interesting reading; but I started with Joan Grant's book first, because I'm curious to know about her strange and exciting life, being the gifted psychic that she was from birth. So far, the book is very satisfying; and this brings me to my question. This book nudged me to take out the manuscript of my novel *Cathedral of My Past Lives*, and I'd like your opinion. Is it time now to get this book out there? Am I ready now to edit, polish, and publish it?"

"An unqualified yes. You are ready to face those emotions again. You have grown sufficiently in your own identity to withstand the onslaught of those emotions, and you MUST work on it; if not totally committed, seeing that you always work on several things at once, at least piecemeal until it is ready to publish. It is an important part of your life, and it speaks to reincarnation in a voice that is totally unique. Joan Grant had her voice, and you have yours. Do not compare the two. Your path was much different from hers. She walked the path of the initiate from a very early age, and she was an initiate in her past lives; this qualifies her to speak with total authority on the subject of reincarnation. Your path was a path of self-discovery. Hers was a path of being who she was. This is the distinction, and both paths are invaluable in their gift to human thought. Yes, work on it."

"You know of course that it will awaken those emotions with my past-life lover and what I did to Penny in our past life in Italy; but if you say I'm ready, I have no reason to doubt you. I think I'm ready, and I may just pull it out over the holidays. I want to get into the right creative rhythm before I do, though. When will that happen? After the passing of our friend?"

"Yes. That will be a very moving experience, and very rewarding. You will give a short talk, and it will awaken many to the reality of your path. Do not fret, my friend; I will be there with you, and the light will shine bright. I promise you."

"Thank you. That's all I needed to hear. Until the next time…"

9. A Feeling of Peace Came Over Me

Friday, December 26, 2014

"Yesterday morning at 7 o'clock, a feeling of peace came over me and I knew that Alice had died. "She's at peace now," I said to myself, and just then Penny came into my writing den for our morning coffee together. I shared my feelings with her, and later that day Alice's brother Fred called and informed me that Alice did pass away at 7 o'clock in the morning; but no-one had contacted me until Fred called. I had told Alice's son to call me when she passed, but he didn't. There's a reason for this, but I won't get into it here. So, Padre; Alice's drama has come to an end, and she's at peace with the choice she made. That's what's important, and I am going to write a eulogy and title it "Honoring Alice's Choice." I need your counsel on this, because it goes to the very heart of the spiritual journey. Your input will be invaluable, since you know this journey so well. What advice can you offer?"

"Your friend is at peace, and she appreciates very much the last words you spoke to her. She knows now why you are the way you are, and her love for you is boundless. She thanks you from the bottom of her heart. She wants to hug you, if you will let her—"

"Right now?"

"Yes."

"Yes, by all means…"

"Alice thanks you and wishes you God's blessing, as you wished her. Now she understands the freedom you gave her to walk her own path. She is much more appreciative of your path now that she has crossed over, and would like to inform you that the world you are going to enter as you continue your journey through life will be more rewarding than you can imagine. That's her parting gift to you."

"Thank you, Alice. All I can do is my best. Now I have to concentrate on my eulogy. I have to get it right, and I think I am going to write it down. I will do an active imagination on it first, or later, and combine the wisdom of both efforts; what do you say, Padre?"

"Yes, by all means; do an active imagination, because this taps you into a source of creative energy that encompasses the consciousness of the experience before it has happened. It's one of those parallel world things that you are going to become more conscious of as you progress in your own journey. I will watch over your progress and make sure it comes out the way it should."

"I specifically request that you caution me from going negative in any manner. Let me accent the joy of Alice's passing."

"Then begin with that in your eulogy. State in no uncertain terms that you are accenting the joy of her passing, not the sadness. That will take everyone by surprise and set the mood for your eulogy."

"I feel strongly nudged to start writing it now. What do you say?"

"By all means. Begin, with my blessing."

"And so I shall. Thank you, Padre.

"You're welcome...."

10. A Word of Counsel, Please?

Monday, December 29, 2014

"Padre, I need a word of counsel. I finished writing my eulogy, which I am now calling a tribute rather than a eulogy; but when I contacted the Eck cleric who is going to be conducting the service for Alice and asked if I could read my tribute, requesting twenty to twenty-five minutes, she balked instantly because she had guidelines that she had to follow for the Eck service. And she wanted to know if I could highlight what I wanted to say and send it to her first, which was an old pattern that I had faced with her before—she wanted to censor my words in case it didn't fit in with the Eck teachings. I reacted and said no; but after I calmed down I asked if I could read my tribute after the service, and she said she would have to contact Alice's ex-husband who was executor of her will. And so we left it at that. Then I called Alice's son and he said it was okay, but I have to ask you something Padre; why the resistance from my spiritual community?"

"You threaten them. You have too much integrity to be contained by the rules of your spiritual community. You have transcended your community, and you are much too free to be contained by the thoughts of your community. Do not fret, my friend; all will go smoothly at the service. I promise you.

"I put my heart into my tribute to Alice, and wanted everyone to hear about Alice's sacred journey; I do hope that I'm given the opportunity."

"After the service, you will read your tribute. It will blow them away. Do not concern yourself about how your spiritual community will react to you and your tribute. It is so well balanced that it would only show their prejudice if they react negatively. I love the tribute that you wrote, and your friend loves and respects you for it. It spoke to her heart, and she thanks you deeply."

"This whole thing has inspired a new spiritual musing, which I'm going to call "Misoneism," which means the fear of the new and strange. I'd like to write it today, but I think I'll wait till after Alice's funeral service which will be tomorrow at one of the funeral homes in Orillia. Alice's death has caused me to do something about my life. Penny and I had to go out on Boxing Day to buy some new clothes for the funeral. I'm overweight and don't fit my old pants, and I had to buy a new pair of dress casuals, and I bought a sweater. I wanted to buy a sports jacket, shirt, tie, and pants; but I went the sweater route instead. I hope I look okay. I want to look comfortable when I'm reading my tribute to Alice. Gosh, Padre; why can't I get my act together?"

"Your energies have been spent elsewhere, but perhaps after your friend's service you can take stock of your life and do something about your weight, and prepare yourself for the next funeral, because there will always be another one."

"Not so soon, I hope. I hate funerals almost as much as I hate going to weddings. You know why I hate going to weddings, and perhaps I'll get over my self-created fear; but for now I have to deal with my life as it is, and I want to get my life in order. The years are rolling in fast, and I pray I'll have enough time to get out the books I want to get out. But all the same, I want to work something out with your help; something about the way I feel today. I can't help but feel that what I am doing is going to blow away like sand in the winds of life, and this scares me into creative paralysis. I hate this state. I want to free myself of this feeling. What can I do about it? Any advice will be greatly appreciated."

"Every writer suffers from this state you call creative paralysis. It's brought on by the feeling of insecurity. It doesn't matter how successful a writer is, the very nature of their discipline calls for total self-confidence; but it's impossible to sustain total self-confidence every hour of every day. It's best to deal with it by diving into your writing without thinking about posterity. Just WRITE!"

"I know that this works, because whenever I am writing I feel filled with creative acknowledgement of my own worth, and this feeling thwarts all those feelings of insecurity. So I guess that's what I'm going to have to do."

"Padre, I may come into some friction from some members of my spiritual community tomorrow. Will you be by my side to thwart off any tension, please?"

"There will be slight tension, but nothing to worry about. Your tribute will go a long way to smooth the waters of your spiritual community."

"Speaking of my spiritual community, the thought occurred to me to not have a service when I pass over; just a gathering of friends. What do you think?"

"In the fullness of time, things will run their course."

"What about my family? My young niece. I feel that I have slighted her with our last conversation. I hope not."

"You always give her much to think about. She's still processing. Give her time. You will be talking in the New Year and will get on in a much more satisfying way, because she will understand you much better."

"If I may, I'd like to switch to another topic. I'm reading Robert Moss's book *The Boy Who Died and Came Back*, and I'm fascinated by what he calls "dream archeology." But the more I read Robert Moss, as exciting and informative as he is (I've read three of his other books: *Active Dreaming*, *The Secret History of Dreaming*, and *The Three "Only" Things*), I'm quickly coming to the conclusion that way of the dream is just another way to one's self, and when one gets there—as all paths will get one there eventually—one then must become his own path; he becomes, to use your phase, "the sum of all spiritual paths." What do you think? Am I on the right track here, because I don't want to get pulled into the way of dreaming; I just don't have the time nor energy to delve into this path. I just want to live my life as a writer, because that is my path. What do you say?"

"I say that you are right on the money. Your life is your path, and your life is writing; so don't fret any more about other paths, even your spiritual community. If I may take the liberty to inform you, your day tomorrow will unfold with the grace of divine providential guidance. No ripples. No tensions. No worries. If you get to read your tribute, fine; if not, fine. You will read it in a parallel world. This is your new reality. It is all one reality, and you are going to be master of the Now. That is your spiritual path. Master of the Now!"

"When do I begin training?"

"Your apprenticeship began with Healing with Padre Pio. That was your initiation into the divine mystery of Now."

"I'd like some formal training. When does that begin?"

30

"Now. Do not smother yourself with thoughts of what might happen. Do not let your mind run your life. Let go of all those thoughts. I am going to give you an exercise that will help anchor you in the Now. Close your eyes every so often every now and then and think of the most wonderful moment of your life. You must choose a different moment each time. When you have chosen that moment, fix it in your mind and relive that moment. This will help anchor you in the Now."

"I see where this is going. Thank you, Padre; until the next time."

"You're welcome, my friend."

11. The Man of God Walks Alone

Wednesday, December 31, 2014

"Well, Padre; I got to read "Honoring Alice's Choice," my tribute to Alice, after the short service yesterday officiated by a cleric of Alice's spiritual path, the New Age religion of the Light and Sound of God, and Alice's family appreciated it very much. In fact, one final coincidence that I will explain later added to the tribute which will bring my book *The Pearl of Great Price* to holy closure. I'll tell you now, if I may.

"When the funeral home printed up the memorial card with Alice's picture and bio, they had Alice's picture on the front of the card correct; but on the inside they had printed a different name from Alice. They had printed the name PEARL. The family noticed the mistake and had to have the cards reprinted. After I read my tribute to Alice, which focussed on Christ's parable of the pearl of great price and Alice's dream of the pearl and the coin, Alice's ex-husband Thayer came up to me to share the bizarre coincidence. Cathy, Alice's sister, was there to confirm the final coincidence to Alice's sacred journey to her divine self. Here's how I interpreted the coincidence for Alice's family. Alice's name and picture were on the outside (her outer self) and the name Pearl was on the inside (her inner, divine self); and that summed up and confirmed my tribute to Alice, that she had won the pearl of great price. Wasn't that a phenomenal coincidence, Padre?"

"Much more than even you realize. It was divinely ordained, and it was meant for the family to witness. It will be the most fitting end to your book, and it will be a towering example of the Voice of God. I'm very happy that you got to read your tribute. It opened up a lot of eyes that did not want to be opened. You did chase the elephant out of the room. It needed to be removed. People went home rethinking their values. You put the fear of God into many people in that room."

"That wasn't my intention. My intention was to honor Alice's choice, because her choice was sacred, and that had to be acknowledged and respected."

"And it was. You did your friend proud."

"Would you like to know what I learned about my whole experience yesterday? I learned that the man of God walks alone. That became clear to me when not one member of my own spiritual community came up to comment on my tribute to one of their own. That was disgusting, because they profess to be all about love. Padre, I know that you are not a big fan of hypocrisy, but that's what I witnessed yesterday—the hypocrisy of human nature; and my feelings about the whole service and reception and the feelings I got from the people on my tribute was summed up in the words that just came to me while relaxing in my recliner at home last night—THE MAN OF GOD WALKS ALONE. I think you know exactly what I mean."

"The journey of the self is long and hard, and the point will come when one walks alone with God. That's the journey that your friend Alice was on, and that's the journey that you acknowledged with your tribute; and although some of the people at the reception saw it, it was too much for them to take in. But yes, you are correct to say that the man of God walks alone. We all do eventually, and we dare not think about it for the fear of being alone. But one is not alone. One walks with God. That is the irony of the journey. I'm very proud of you, my friend. You did your duty to Alice, and you did her proud. She was standing by your side while you were reading, watching everyone's reactions. She learned a great deal from their reactions. She was both amused and disappointed."

"I did push a few buttons, didn't I?"

"Not intentionally. Your focus was honoring Alice's choice, and however that effected people was determined by their feelings alone."

"Padre, how would you describe a person who walks alone with God?"

"Courageous. Honest. Uncompromising. Bold. Daring. Compassionate. Unwilling to sacrifice their belief to please others. The man who walks with God is a man who risks the world. He walks in the footsteps of all the giants of the world, acknowledged or not by the world. The man who walks with God walks at peace with himself,

because he has paid the price that he was called to pay. The man who walks with God walks alone because he leaves the world behind. The man who walks with God has made a choice to walk with God and not the world. That is what sets him apart from the world. He is alone because he chooses God over the world. This is the hardest part of the journey of the self; but it is a journey that every person will one day have to make. Your friend Alice was on this journey, and you acknowledged it with your tribute. It will make a great book. I promise!"

"Thank you. And now to another piece of news. Last night, after we got settled in after our trying day at the service, we got a phone call from the daughter of one of our tenants that has been living in the middle apartment of our triplex up north for the past ten years or so and she told us that her mother is going into a nursing home, so we will be losing our tenant at the end of January. We are sad to see her go, but we know that it is the best thing for her. Padre, can you please get us another great tenant? Or, better still, can you find us a buyer for our triplex?"

"Your concern is to be expected, but do not fear. Your life is on a different trajectory, and the way has been made clear for you. I promise."

"I wish you would be more specific, but I trust you Padre; so thank you for your love and understanding. I'm not up to talking any more, but I had to tell you about yesterday's experience. I got one final coincidence to bring holy closure to my book *The Pearl of Great Price*, and the whole ordeal was worth it just for that alone, because that speaks to the authenticity of my tribute. I wanted to honor Alice's choice, and the divine law of synchronicity honored it with one final coincidence that summed up the whole theme of my book *The Pearl of Great Price*. We are our human personality on the outside, but we are the pearl of great price on the inside; and that's what Alice's sacred journey to her divine self attested to. That's why I had to honor her choice. I had to, Padre. I had no choice."

"That was obvious by the intensity of your emotions, which everyone picked up on; and this made your friend Alice very, very proud. She thanks you again for your tribute, and she promises me she's going to watch over you."

"Thank you Alice. If I may, what does Alice think of her spiritual community now? Does she see where I am coming from now?"

"She understands completely why you feel as you do about your spiritual community, and she welcomes your understanding with an open heart. She sees why you no longer participate, and why you will be leaving your community; but she does not judge them. She sees them for what they are, and she lets them work things out on their own. But she is disappointed that no-one spoke for her except you, who were the least among them. This both pleased and disappointed her."

"And none of her co-workers spoke for her. I think I pushed a button there, didn't I? I think Alice noticed and was appreciative of my tribute for that reason alone. She wanted them to know why she chose the way she did, and they did find out; but to their total surprise, because Alice's choice was beyond them."

"Exactly. Only you could see her choice from the spiritual point of view. That's why you were called upon to write The Pearl of Great Price."

"Padre, I trust your words implicitly; but please, could you relieve me of the fear that now attends me because of losing our tenant?"

"Ask no more of this. It is already taken care of, to your credit. You need not worry about tomorrow, because the way has been cleared for you and your loved one. As I have told you, you are on a different trajectory now. You are on the path of the alone to the Alone, and that is the path of the realized soul."

"This confirms my feelings about all other paths, like Robert Moss's path of the way of dreaming; it's just another path that will take him to the path of the alone to the Alone; the path that crosses all bridges to the path of the realized soul."

"Well said. Now don't worry about tomorrow. Tomorrow will take care of itself. I promise you."

"Thank you, Padre."

"You're welcome, my good friend. Until we talk again..."

12. Thoughts for the New Year

Thursday, January 1, 2015

"Well, here we are again, the first day of a New Year; so, if I may take a moment before we begin our talk this morning, the first one of the New Year, let me wish you the most satisfying New Year, and may your mission, however you define it, be the most fruitful of all the years you have been on your mission. That is my New Year's wish for you. And may our dialogues be so rich in textured truth and understanding and compassion and love that I will grow into the wholeness of my divine nature as you have grown in yours, and more I hear you say. So, good morning Padre. Let's jump right into our first talk of the New Year—"

"Thank you. And may your New Year bring you the richness you deserve, spiritually, emotionally, intellectually, and financially; and may your health be sound and joyful that you may continue your mission to satisfactory closure. I wish you and your loved one the most satisfying New Year of your life. That is my wish for you, my good friend. Now, what would you like to talk about to begin our dialogues for the New Year?"

"I would like to ask for your guidance for my book *The Pearl of Great Price*. I was given the ending for my book with Alice's sacred journey, and I would love to bring this book to closure before spring. I want it to be as good as I can possibly make it, and better if that is possible. And I would like our dialogues to take me to new heights of spiritual growth and awareness."

"The Pearl of Great Price will be one of your most treasured books, and it will open many eyes. Your journey to your true self is a very sacred journey, because it crosses so many frontiers; and I would be honored to assist you, because the pearl of great price was my most treasured parable. I knew what the pearl was also, and I made myself see the pearl in every person that I talked to. The pearl of great price gave me the strength to believe in the goodness of man,

and whenever I felt doubt about my fellow man I always went back to the pearl of great price. So, yes; your book will do wonders for the teachings of Jesus Christ. You must go back to the Gospels and refresh your memory. You will need that to complete your book. And please, do not fear letting the moving finger write. It is your strongest suite as a creative writer, because your Muse has much to say to the world."

"I'm thinking of fleshing in my first chapter."

"Yes, I see it fleshed in. You will give it the more personal touch, which will pull in the reader much more. By all means, go back and refresh your chapter. Just let the moving finger write."

"I can hear you almost scolding me to trust my own judgement. I have questions that I am afraid to ask you, but you answer them by telling me to trust my own judgement. I know what you mean, but I am afraid to bring it out into the open; but can I write about what I feel? I have to, don't I? Because this is what my sacred journey is all about, isn't it?"

"You have transcended your own voice, and the voice of your spiritual community; and not until you accept this fully will you be free to write what your heart knows to be the truth. You have outgrown your life and are now on a different level of awareness. The person you were, you are no longer; and to explain this I would have to go deep into the mysteries. But not now. For now you must draw upon the energy of your own doubt, and overcome your doubt by writing through it. Doubt is a source of great creative energy when you seek to understand. You have seen through the 'shtick,' as you call it, of one of the authors you have discovered (Jean Houston), *and you have seen through the illusions of those who cannot break free of the hold their mind has over them (the sceptics), and no longer need to be validated by anyone because you have outgrown the teachings of the world and are deep into the mystery of your own sacred journey; so let the moving finger write."*

"I've changed the title of this book. It's now called *The Man of God Walks Alone.* I think I explained that to you yesterday. Gosh, that seems like so long ago. This is good. When time slows down for me, I get more out of life. So, about our talks; when are they going to open up? When will I feel the objectivity of your presence in our talks, and not just a deeper expression of myself?"

"That's a wonderful question. But didn't you hear Jean Houston quote the Christian mystic Meister Eckhart yesterday who said that the "I" of man and the "I" of God are one and the same "I"? Does that answer your question?"

"It's all about trust, isn't it? I have to learn to trust myself. To trust the creative process. To trust God. I have to just let the moving finger write; is that it?"

"Yes. The more you trust, the more you will be given. It is the law of the creative process. Ask any highly creative person and they will tell you that when they abandon to their Muse they go places they could not have imagined. That's what Jung had to do. He had to let go and trust his unconscious, and the result changed his life and the lives of many, many people."

"Am I to gather that TRUST is my byword for the year 2015?"

"Yes. Trust God. Trust yourself. Trust your Muse."

"The Holy Trinity—God, myself, and my Muse!"

"The Father, the Son, and the Holy Ghost. Beautiful, my friend!"

"And so it begins, then. God willing, I will go back to work on *The Pearl of Great Price* today. I think I'm going to try and flesh in chapter one, "The Inspiration for My Story." I want to bring it closer to the reader."

"By all means. Read the whole manuscript first, and then go back to chapter one and flesh it in. You will know what to write. I promise you."

"Thank you, Padre. Until we talk again, then."

"Live, love, and enjoy your life; that is my New Year's wish for you and your loved one. Have a great day, my dear friend..."

13. Much Better than I Expected

Tuesday, February 10, 2015

"I'm glad to report that I just finished writing *The Pearl of Great Price*, and it turned out much better than I expected. I know you were standing by my side as I wrote it, and I thank you for your guidance. I did not expect that final coincidence, though; it took me completely by surprise. Wasn't that something?"

"It certainly was. It came as a surprise to me, if you can believe that—"

"No, I can't. But I suspect you have an explanation."

"Yes, I do. When I'm working with you, I have to respect the unfolding of your life according to your own design; and the coincidence of Alice's memorial card was born of the inevitable momentum of your special relationship with Alice. Spirit saw fit to bless you with that final coincidence, because it not only brought healing grace to Alice's family, but brought convincing closure to your story."

"But you can step back from my life and into the consciousness of all knowing and seeing; right?"

"Yes, I can and do. It's a very curious state, but I think you understand perfectly how this process works. You're becoming quite intuitive."

"Did you guide me to Jean Houston's talk for my very short afterward for *The Pearl of Great Price*?"

"Yes. I felt that the book needed rounding off. It seemed like the reader was left wanting. Don't you think it works well?"

"I think it's perfect. Like a nice after-dinner espresso."

"Now I'm going to read my manuscript and edit and tighten it, and I invite you to come along for the ride. I like being nudged by you. It seems to work, for some reason. I'd really like one day to visit your birth village of Pietrelcino and San Giovanni Rotondo where you lived most of your life; but it's not really necessary. It would be nice, but I no longer have a compelling urge. Maybe it will happen now that I don't have the need. That's how it usually works, doesn't it?"

"More often than not. Keep your hopes up. It may just happen."

"Padre, I'm low on creative energy. I was up at three this morning. If you don't mind, I'd like to shut down for today. Maybe tomorrow after my edit I'll have more creative energy for a longer chat. Okay?"

"By all means. Until tomorrow, then…"

14. Back to Words

"Good morning, Padre. I just noticed that today is Friday 13th, and I don't know what to make of that. Is it going to be an unlucky day? Or is the day going to unfold according to the dynamic of my life's agenda?"

"A very good question. So, good morning my friend. Before we get too far involved in whatever Divine Spirit has in mind for us, let me congratulate you on your new book The Pearl of Great Price. *Yes, you are quite correct to see it as an accomplishment in light of all the people that you have read that sought to solve the problems of the self; your book has provided an answer that will take the pressure off the human psyche. One of man's greatest needs is to know himself, after he's had the luxury of many lifetimes to question the meaning and purpose of life, and your book provides an answer that goes to the heart of the problem. There is no other book like this in the world. It is the distilled essence of life's wisdom as lived by you, and because of your own experiences to your true self the book takes on the energy of the creative writer—like good novels should. But your story is true. And to add the story of your friend Alice's sacred journey is icing on the cake. I am very proud of you for writing this book. Very, very proud."*

"Thank you. And as to the unfolding of my Friday 13th. How is it going to unfold, according to superstition or according to the agenda of my life?"

"The trajectory of your life is to complete you spiritual mission, which supersedes superstition. So you have no need to fear. Your life is in the hands of your spiritual mission, and the laws of one's destiny transcend the laws of life. This is a mystery that you will grow into."

"I suspect I know the answer already, because I've always suspected that great souls like Winston Churchill and Abraham Lincoln were men of destiny, and it just seemed to me that the laws of life didn't apply to them. They seemed to be spared the indignities of the ordinary mortal. Is that what you're hinting at?"

"Yes. Men of destiny are old souls that have returned to life to serve humanity, and the laws of life arranges for them to fulfill their mission."

"From my place of understanding today, I have the freedom to see life so much more objectively than I used to. I was very subjective in my understanding of life before I had my spiritual healing sessions with you, and after I wrote the books I did after my spiritual healing I seemed to have transcended the dual nature of the human personality—to that place of objective awareness where I can see both sides of man at once. It's quite the place to be, which is your place of all knowing and seeing; not that I am in that place with you, but I've got a taste of it. And what a relief it is to no longer see life in black and white, but in that perpetual phase of becoming the one or the other. And with luck, both combined. Are you following my thought?"

"Perfectly. That's the spiritual state of consciousness. It's where Soul resides, in the higher planes of human thought. That's why our books after your spiritual healing have taken on the objective truth of life as opposed to the subjective truth before your spiritual healing, and they are much more fun to read."

"Now, as to my newfound interest in words. I've taken out some old books on vocabulary, because I seem to have a need to expand my powers of expression which I can only do with an expanded vocabulary. What's with this?"

"Words are the carriers of thought, and your thought power needs all the words you can harness to give expression to them. It is a natural need born of your newfound state of objectivity. By all means, learn new words and expand your vocabulary. It will titillate your learning muscles and excite your imagination. It is necessary for your own growth and understanding."

"Here's a question I have to ask you: am I correct in my perception that the world has many souls that have evolved to the objective level of being both but neither of their lower aspects of their self, of being their Soul Self? I don't think I expressed that very well. What I'm trying to say is that I have come to believe that there are souls in the world that have completed their karmic destiny and are now serving life from their higher state of spiritual consciousness. Do you see what I'm trying to say?"

"Yes. These are the great souls that have returned to serve life out of love for humanity. There are more of these high souls than you realize."

"And what about my understanding that life is perfect as it is? Doesn't this throw a whole new light on the human condition?"

"It certainly does. It makes sense of the human condition in a way that no one else has been able to explain. You need to do a spiritual musing on this thought. It will go a long way to explaining the misery of the human condition."

"Yes, I've been tapped on the shoulder already by my Muse. I have half a dozen spiritual musings waiting for me to write. But I have the feeling that these new musings are going to be different. Are they?"

"Your book The Pearl of Great Price has granted you the privilege of a lifetime. You have gained entry into the secret domain of sacred knowledge, and it will pour out of you at will when you write from here on in. Your spiritual musings will take on an objectivity that will be refreshingly frightening, and so informative us to liberate many souls trapped by their own mind."

"That's what writing with an *enlightened attitude* does, doesn't it?"

"Yes. The enlightened attitude is not easy to come by, though; as you've indicated with your book The Pearl of Great Price. But once one has earned their enlightened attitude, they affect life in a different way. Watch your writing from this day on and you will see what I am talking about."

"Actually, I glad to have completed *The Pearl of Great Price.* It freed me from an inner obligation that was beginning to bother me. In my freedom, I feel like I've gained something that I cannot quite explain yet; but I feel it has to do with having much greater access to sacred knowledge. Is this true?"

"Yes. Sacred knowledge comes with one's initiation, and as one fulfills his spiritual mission in life one is granted greater access. This is the Way of Soul, the higher path of man's journey through life. All great souls walk this path."

"And I need to expand my vocabulary to give better expression to the rest of my journey, *n'est-ce pas?*"

"Yes. That's why you've been called to expand your vocabulary. And also to excite your curiosity and imagination. They need new excitement."

"Okay, Padre; I have to get to work now. I'm editing *The Pearl* and would like to have it ready to print up for Penny to read this weekend. Thank you for the chat. I hope to do more of this when I'm done my editing."

"You're welcome…"

15. When Interest Wanes, Love Does Too

Saturday, February 14, 2015

"Hi Padre. I'd like to chat for a moment or two, if you don't mind."

"Not at all. What did you have in mind?"

"I posted a new spiritual musing for my blog. It's called "If Only," the two saddest words in the world. I got some reaction, but not what I expected. To be honest, I don't expect much reaction to my blog anymore. I seem to have stepped too far beyond the interest of those readers, or something like that. Do you have an explanation?"

"Not too far. You are still in the running. So much so that the gravitas of your writing is gaining momentum. It will draw you readers, more than you will ever imagine; but you must be patient. It is coming, I promise."

"I got a thought as I sat down to chat with you. The thought that came to me wasn't of my doing. I think it came from you. It was this: "when interest wanes, love does too." This thought came because today is Valentine's Day. I was going to go out to get Penny roses and a card, but I was feint in my desire; and the thought came to me that when I lose interest, I lose love. Was that you?"

"Yes and no. It was your inner self, and your inner self is Soul; and Soul is you and me and everybody. This is the mystery of your life and writing. So, what are you going to do?"

"Go out and get some roses and a Valentine card, of course; and perhaps a Valentine cake. That should make Penny happy. So, if you don't mind, Padre; I'm going to change and do what I'm called to do—by my Higher Self!"

"Have a good day, my friend..."

"Thank you..."

16. What's Going On, Padre?

Tuesday, February 17, 2015

"My energies are split. I'm a little concerned. I did a final edit to my book *The Pearl of Great Price* yesterday and printed up a copy for Penny to read and edit, but the energy in the house changed once I handed her the manuscript, and I'd like to know what's going on? Does it have to do with my book? I ask because I believe the energy of my book is so high and intense that it even affected my printer when I printed it out yesterday. Is this fantasy on my part, or is there any truth to my suspicion"

"And good morning to you, my friend—"

"Sorry, Padre. I got carried away. I'm a little beside myself and don't quite know which writing project to pour myself into—spiritual musings, short stories, one of my novels, or just chat with you; I'm at a loss as to what to do. And I'm also fretting about my weight and whether or not I should start doing some exercises, but some fear keeps me from getting started. I think I have a resistance for reasons which I can't quite fathom. Perhaps I have a death wish. I do look forward to getting out of this world, so perhaps I want to help myself cross over by not paying attention to my health as I should. Not that I am that neglectful; I just don't have that interest in my physical health as I used to. I'm fighting myself for some reason. Can you give me an explanation? I'd really like to know."

"You're very close to the truth. Yes, you do want out of this life, and you do resist getting more fit; but that's for reasons which go deep into your past lives. You do have an aversion to healthy living, even though you were very fit in your youth and tried to keep fit. You want to prove something to yourself. You want to prove that your life is in the hands of the 'choreographers,' to use your word. You want to make your point that your life is pre-determined, and determined—a paradox that only you can grasp because it is beyond the mind of most people; and this saps you of the all your initiative to exercise and get fit. That's the explanation. It's not a death wish. It's a life

wish. You want to live, but on terms that you can't quite fathom—is it on your terms, or on the 'choreographers' terms?"

"So I'm in a kind of stasis state of life, then? My mind is stuck between doing and not doing, is that it?"

"Practically speaking, yes. You have to break out of this non-productive pattern to get your life where you would like it to be."

"How?"

"Confront the reality of your situation. You believe in free will, and you believe in the 'choreographers' of life—the spiritual agency, if you will, that guide your life; but your free will and this spiritual agency are not on opposite sides of the fence. They are both you, and you have to reconcile this reality in your mind. That's how you can break out of your stasis state of consciousness."

"I sense a depth of pride on my part, because it's like I'm challenging this spiritual agency to do me in; is that it?"

"Yes. That would liberate you from what you perceive to be the pressures of daily living. You are a tired soul, my good friend; and this is something that I know very well. You and I are very much alike. This is why we get along so well. And to answer your unasked question, I worked my way through my insecurity by praying to my lord and savior Jesus. I prayed and prayed and prayed."

"I know. I read enough biographies on your life to see how much time you spent praying. You prayed so deeply that you wept so much that it left stains on the floor where you prayed. That's praying! But did it help you resolve your fear?"

"In all honesty, not quite. I prayed because I didn't know what else to do. And then it occurred to me to pray for other people. I would think of a particular penitent and pray for them. That's why I prayed so much. I prayed for my penitents."

"And did that help remove your fear or did it just deflect it?"

"A little of both. But let's get back to you. How do you plan to resolve your quandary? You have to get over this to complete your mission."

"My mission? My writing, you mean?"

"Your writing is born of your mission. Your mission is to transcend yourself to your highest potential. That's the mission of every soul. But you have initiated the process and you understand the process; that's what makes you different."

"Back to my book, then. *The Pearl of Great Price* has a lot of energy. Was it responsible for my printer acting up, and the change of energy in the house once I got it printed? Is that fantasy or reality?"

"You are not wrong to believe that your book is packed with energy of a very high spiritual nature, and yes, it has changed the energy of your house. It was also responsible for your printer acting up. But the energy is harmonizing now, and will continue to do so. And when Penny finishes reading the book your house will be operating on a much higher level of spiritual consciousness. This is the natural consequence of releasing your energy into the world. As a point of interest, keep an eye on your loved one. See how your book affects her outlook on life. Be patient with her, because your book packs a powerful punch."

"I will. Now, if I may ask; I've been called back to my book of short stories, *Enantiodromia*. This is what you have always wanted me to do—write stories from the heart. Am I to go in this direction? I feel torn, because I've also been called to my novel *Cathedral of My Past Lives.*"

"My preference for you at this time would be your book of short stories. You have much to say in your stories, and your material will be fresh. I would spend the next two or three months completing that book. It will be richly rewarding."

"I still fear writing those stories though."

"I know. That's why I prefer that you write it before you go back to your other novels. You will get to them, I promise you; but you have to resolve the issue of your fear of writing from the heart. That's your biggest problem. You have an issue with those deep emotions that you keep resisting; but story writing will get you there."

"I'd like to open up in my short stories. Can you tell me how?"

"Read short stories while your write your stories. Reading short stories by accomplished authors will open you up. Alice Munroe, Mavis Gallant, Anton Chekov, John Updike, read collections of classic short stories—this is how you will open up, naturally like a rose. It's the process of taking in what you want to put out. It's always been the natural way of learning. Trust yourself to the process."

"I may start with a collection of classic short stories. What do you say?"

"That would be an excellent place to start. But don't try to read all the stories you can just so you can put off writing your own stories. You must write your stories as you read short stories. It has to be a combined endeavor. You can learn to play chess why reading about playing chess, if I may express it this way."

"I have some titles for short stories that excite me. I got an idea the other day to write a second story based on the friend we had over for dinner Saturday. What do you think? And perhaps a story on the funeral that I attended for my friend Alice, for whom I wrote my tribute. And one or two other stories drawn from my experience of my spiritual community. Should I explore that further?"

"Trust your Muse."

"I think I got a solution to my stasis quandary. I should strive for an ideal, regardless of the 'choreographer' of my life. By striving for an ideal—what I would like to be in my mind's eye—I will draw inspiration to DO; and, as you say, DOING is the answer to life's problems. We have to DO in order to BE. So, to be the ideal that I would like to be, I have to DO. Keep my ideal in mind, and just work towards the realization of my ideal. Is it that simple?"

"Yes. You will be amazed at the results from the simple act of DOING. You don't have to climb Everest in one effort. It takes time to get to the top of the mountain; and so it will take time to realize your IDEAL. But how else to get there but by DOING. This is the answer to resolving most of life's quandaries."

"I'd like to ask you about a thought I had the other day. The thought came to me while reading an article in the paper about the law that was passed in Canada allowing doctor-assisted suicide. This article stressed that now severely depressed people may find a way to legal suicide, and the thought came to me that since the severely depressed person is at their rope's end, why not try past-life regression therapy. It just seemed to me given my belief in the shadow self of man that past lives would have a lot to do with one's depression, and quite possibly regression might get to the root of the problem. What do you think?"

"Past lives play a much greater role in one's current life than people will ever realize. It is going to be the healing science of the future, and you are quite right to believe that depression is past-life related. And just by putting the thought out there is a good place to

start. And your thought of writing a story on a regression that helps to cure one's depression wouldn't be a bad idea. It would require some reading on depression, but that's all available on the Internet."

"Do you think it would work in my book *Enantiodromia*?"

"That's the thought, isn't it?"

"I guess we'll have to wait and see. Now, I think I'm going to work on my spiritual musing 'Gerbils of the Mind' that I started the other day. I'd like to get into that before I lose the thread of that thought. So, Padre; thank you for the chat this morning. It got me slightly out of my funk. Maybe by working on my musing I can get myself the rest of the way out. Give me a boost, if you would. I need all the help I can get, and you are quite handy. By the way, I have a feeling that the next time we chat through the psychic who channeled you for my novel *Healing with Padre Pio* we're going to be getting into some very interesting material, like my parallel life which I suspect is responsible for many of my dreams. There's much more to this concept of living my same life over again that I haven't grasped, and I think we're going to explore that. Are we?"

"There is much to say about living one's same life over again. This is an aspect of reincarnation that hasn't been touched upon yet. You are going to be the first writer to deal with it on a personal level."

"Are we going to explore it together?"

"Yes."

"When I'm ready to explore it?"

"You're ready now, but you have other books to write first."

"Okay. Until next time, then…"

17. Honoring "It"

Wednesday, February 18, 2015

"I didn't do any writing yesterday. I didn't feel like it. Instead I watched three or four shows of Kavenaugh QC, starring John Thaw. I love that show. It's a British drama, and I watched it on You Tube; but I've run out of shows to watch. I may have to start watching Inspector Morse, also starring John Thaw. Something about this actor fascinates me. He's true through and through, and he brings that to his characters Kavenaugh and Inspector Morse. In any event, I'm telling you this because I feel a bit guilty for not writing yesterday. I feel I wasted, or almost wasted my day. I did feel I gained something from watching those shows, and for that I absolve myself of any guilt I may have for not writing; but I thought I'd share that with you because you do have that effect on me. By this I mean that being the Father Confessor of so many penitents, you would understand where I'm coming from."

"I do, and I forgive you; if that's what you're looking for. You know very well that you are your own confessor, but it's always good to hear it from another. That's human nature. We all need to be forgiven for our perceived sins. It's always been, because it's natural for man to know himself better than others. Conscience is a personal thing, and it cannot be weighed and measured by another. This was the lesson that I learned as Father Confessor. The deepest sins we commit are known only to the sinner, and only he can work them out. That's why it takes great courage to go to confession, and why I took my role as Father Confessor so seriously. I was judge and jury for my penitents, and that wasn't an easy role to take. But I wanted to be a priest from my youth, and I wanted to be a forgiver of sins. That was my calling. I am telling you this to acquaint you with the art of reading another's soul. It is much more difficult than people realize, because the soul of a person is the history of the person's entire life— and many lives, if we want to extend the paradigm to include soul's entire history. And the way to read another person's soul is to know

one's own soul first. This is why writing stories from the heart is good for you. It is an excellent way to explore your own soul. Need I say more?"

"No. Is that why I like the actor John Thaw? His character Kavenaugh, and Inspector Morse?"

"Kavenaugh more than Morse, because Kavenaugh is the more evolved. He's Morse put through the mill of life, as it were. Yes, that's why you like this man's acting. He brought a lot of himself into those roles."

"I read from three books this morning. I started with Dr. Brian Weiss's book *Through Time Into Healing*, then I read from John Updike's *More Matter, Essays and Criticism*, and then I read from Joseph Campbell's *The Hero with a Thousand Faces* to learn more about the hero's journey; and then I thought I was going to start working on my spiritual musing "Gerbils of the Mind," but I decided to chat with you a while just to prime the pump, as it were. I hope you don't mind. Of course, you know that I'm just putting off my writing because I don't feel like doing the serious thinking that's required of me to write my spiritual musing; but I will get to it eventually. Hopefully, after Penny goes to work."

"It's all a process, and how it unfolds it unfolds. Do not place too much importance on it, because that will only curb your enthusiasm. Just let it happen without judgment. That's the key to a happy life."

"As long as one is in a position to just let it happen. It would be difficult to do within the constraints of a daily job and responsibilities."

"Not necessarily. In fact, if one learns how to just let it happen without judgement within the paradigms that you mentioned, it would be that much more effective because one would be synchronizing with the forces of life. That's the key to a really happy life."

"Am I being led to that magical place that you called a "karma free life"? Is this what this points to? Because I feel it does. When one is in complete synch with life, where's the karma? Life is the Way, and when one is in synch with the Way, where's the karma? Am onto something here?"

"In theory, yes; but in practice one will never be in total synch with life because one is all too human. One can get close, but to be in total sync with life would mean becoming one with the Divine. That's a long way off for the mystic traveller, despite how holy he may be. The Divine is the Alone, and the Alone is the Alone. If you follow that logic, you know that the alone will always be striving for the Alone, which is never ending. It is a mystery within a mystery. But you have caught a glimpse of this mystery, and it will be a source of great energy for you because it will preserve all of that energy you would otherwise spend trying to resolve it. This is the way it is until it no longer is this way."

"And as I change, the mystery changes?"

"Well said!"

"Where do we go from here, then?"

"We'll continue to explore the mystery. What else can we do?"

"Me incrementally, and you guiding me?"

"If you so desire. I enjoy our little talks. They bring me back to my own life and all the doubts and anxieties that I had, and it's a joy watching you work your way through yours. By all means, let's continue with our talks. You never know what you will learn when we open up to the creative Spirit."

"I have to tell you that I'm still intimidated by John Updike's writing. He has a way of writing that has opened up his mind to the ways of life, and that's magical to me. It's like he has the gift of being another person when he writes; no, that's not it entirely. He can take in a whole life vicariously, so it seems; and then he writes about it from that point of view. I've never read anyone who can be so convincing in his metaphors and insights. They seem to be wrought out of the hard core of life and yet I know he lived a very suburban life. His life was all about trying to capture the essential stuff of life, which he does with gifted passion. He just seems to get "it" even if he doesn't understand "it," if you know what I'm trying to say."

"That's Updike's genius. He does get "it". That's why he's envied by so many writers. But he didn't go with "it" as he could have. That's why Professor Bloom said that he always hovered near greatness. To get "it" is not the same as being "it". The great writers became "it" and were the real thing. Updike was close to the real

thing, but not quite. He got "it" but could not hold "it". That's the mystery of the man's writing. He wrote eloquently about "it"—and perhaps we should explain that "it" is the very core of life, the essence of the life experience—but as much as he tried to honor "it" in his own life, he could not. But he honored "it" with his writing. That's what makes him such a mysterious writer. He came as close as any writer to grasping the essential purpose of "it," but because he failed to honor "it" in his own life, he could only honor "it" in his writing. This is why you love John Thaw's character Kavenaugh, because he honored "it" in his life. And look at what it cost him to honor "it" in his life. He had to fight to honor "it" because it was so easy to dishonor "it". But let's further explain that by "it" we mean the God force that flows through all of life, and lest we honor and revere the God force we are doomed to suffer the agony of incompleteness. This is Updike's greatest fear, and why he was tortured all of his life like his hero Kierkegaard. Becoming "it" requires the greatest sacrifice of all—the sacrifice of one's either/or self. It means becoming both either and or. It means transcending yourself, which can only happen when one honors "it" in all of its demands. This is the hero's journey. And reading from those three books this morning points to the different stages of the hero's journey to his transcendent self. Weiss opens up the reader to the healing power of "it" through one's past life memories, which liberates the individual from the stagnant pools of his own life and allows the hero to continue on his journey to wholeness and transcendence; Updike's essay on the short story that you read tells you how he progresses on his own hero's journey through story writing and lustful reading of literature; and Campbell's book takes the mystery out of the hero's journey by explaining it through the mythologies of the world. So all in all, the "it" that makes up life is what it's all about—if you will allow me the pun."

"Wow! Thank you for that, Padre. Nice way to bring our talk to closure this morning. If I may, until the next time…"

18. Every Story Is the Story of God

Sunday, February 22, 2015

"Inspector Morse died yesterday, in the last episode of the *Inspector Morse* TV drama, and when he died I welled up with tears because I liked the man. He was honest and decent, and when he died I said, 'A life well lived.' Because I liked Inspector Morse (his first name was Endeavor, but he never told anyone and insisted that he simply be called Morse), I looked up the actor John Thaw who played Inspector Morse and came across comments made by his wife and daughters and fellow actors, and they all spoke highly of him. The actor Peter O'Toole said that John Thaw had a 'deep, deep, deep goodness.' I could see that, because he brought that to his character Inspector Morse, and also to his other role as *Kavanagh QC*, a show by the same name that I loved even more than *Inspector Morse*. I'm telling you this Padre, because when I watched Morse die yesterday in what I presumed to be the last episode of *Inspector Morse* which ran on British television for a number of years, I felt a great sense of loss. That's how much that character had worked his way into my life. He made a formidable impression, and his death brought me to tears. And I'd like to talk with you about this, because I think that a life well lived is worth discussing. Don't you?"

"Yes. This is what life should be, well lived. This is how one gets the most benefit from life; but well lived with honesty, decency, and goodness. That's what defined Inspector Morse, and that's what endeared him to his public. The world loves the good and decent, because the world knows how hard it is to be good and decent; and Morse was a knight in shining armor. Goodness and decency were his shield against the forces of life, and Morse inspired his public to be a little better and more decent in their own lives. That was a good show. It provided more than entertainment; it provided inspiration for the good life, and his death was mourned by his public, as you have proven with how his death affected you."

"When I watched *Inspector Morse* and *Kavanagh QC,* I experienced life vicariously. I had two past lives that I know of in England, and those shows seemed to fill some historical void, like they nourished some nostalgic need; is that why I loved those shows, aside from the actor John Thaw and what he brought to his characters—goodness and decency?"

"You lived more than two lives in the British Isles, but that's not necessary for you to know at this time. It will be necessary another time, when you are more in need of that knowledge. Suffice to say that you have a long history that goes deep into the Celtic life, and your nostalgia is legitimate. Those shows satisfied your need to return to the consciousness of your people, but you got what you needed from those lives and moved on; and watching those shows served its purpose of filling that void in your life. You will be attracted to other things, as you always are; because this is how the arc of your life is unfolding."

"Okay, now I think I can get to the nub of my thought this morning. I wanted to work up to it before I jumped into it, and I think I'm ready now: I want to talk about my sense of time and purpose. I don't know how else to express it, but I'm having trouble pinning myself down to the NOW of my life, which deprives me of the satisfaction of the moment. Do you understand what I'm trying to say?"

"Perfectly. You fear dying before finishing what you started. You have a number of books left to write and get out, beside the ones you have already written, and you have so many books you would love to read; and you're afraid of not doing all that you would love to do. That's simple enough. But that's the underlying fear of every life. Every person in the world suffers from this fear. You simply brought it to the surface, that's all. But knowing what your fear is does not take it away. The only thing that will take your fear away is—DOING. This is the cure for your ailment. Just DO and let life unfold as it will. I can assure you that you will not cross over until you have completed your mission, and everything you have to get done you will. It would be unrealistic to say that your dream will be completed in this lifetime, because that's not possible for any life; it will go on, and on, and on because there is no end to the realization of one's spiritual

nature. So don't worry about tomorrow and live your life today. That's the best cure for you."

"Thank you. I always have to be reminded of that. But it was Morse's death that brought it home yesterday. When he died I asked myself if I had lived my life well and will I die with a sense of completeness. Will anyone say, he lived his life well? What will they say, if anyone says anything?"

"Let's not go there. You have years to go before you think like that. Just continue with your writing and reading and let your life unfold. Besides, your books will speak for you, and it is how you feel about your books that counts."

"Let's talk about that, then; not necessarily how I feel about my books, but about what I write and why I write what I write. I've given writing a lot of thought and practice over the years, and I've come to see that story is where the best of literature can be found; because story is the heart and soul of life. That's why you want me to write stories from the heart, isn't it?"

"You have discovered the secret truth of life that few people discover, that life is nothing but STORY. Life is the story of God, and every life tells the story of God in the drama of life's experience. Every story is sacred, because every story is the story of God in that particular moment of time; and how well the story speaks for God determines how well lived that life has been. That's why you cried when Morse died; because you felt how well lived his life had been. Don't fret about what you write. Write your stories and let them speak for themselves. You have found your voice, especially with The Pearl of Great Price, and you need not compare yourself with other writers. You are your own writer, with your own voice; and you goal in life is to get your voice heard through the stories you write. Full stop."

"Then do me a favor and keep my demon fears from fudging up my thoughts and feelings. I don't need that crap in my life!"

"Who does? Yes, I will watch over you. I promise."

"I've started editing my book of stories *Enantiodromia*. I've done four so far, and I'm looking forward to writing the second half of the book. I've got several ideas for stories, and one in particular is starting to take shape. It's a story on Alice's funeral that Penny and I attended. I fear writing it, but I think that's a good fear. I think what when fear for writing a story possess me, it's meant for me to write that story; is that the case?"

"Yes, because when fear to write a story possesses you it means that you have something important to say, something that people have to hear but don't want to; that's what true creative writing is all about. The creative unconscious wants it out there, and your job is to get it out; and by creative unconscious I mean your Higher Self, which is your Soul Self—'God within,' to used Emerson's phrase. This is why every story is the story of God. Simple enough?"

"I'm beginning to see that. And I do love that line—EVERY STORY IS THE STORY OF GOD. Wow!"

"Yes, wow indeed! This should give you more inspiration to write your stories, especially your story on Alice's funeral. Change the names and write the story essentially as it happened, letting your creative unconscious guide you."

"It's going to take me to that place I don't want to go to, though; that place deep in the pocket of my spiritual community—"

"Of course it will. That's the heart of the story. But someone has to tell that story. No one else has the awareness to tell it. It's a good story, and you will not violate the trust you have in your teaching. It's the shadow that you're going to write about. It has too much power over your community. But you can't call it your community anymore, can you? You have moved on. You are on your own path, my friend; and you really have no choice but to write it as it happened, if we may go back to your literary mentor whose literary ethic was to tell it as it happened—Ernest Hemingway, that is. He's still the source of your literary ideal, despite the shadow side of his personality; and he's very proud of you these days. He enjoys reading all of your new books. I promise, you have quite the following over here."

"Why?"

"Because you have broken the code. You know that life is the Way, and everyone who has an interest in the purpose and meaning of life is following your career. You provide a great source of inspiration for many souls, so don't fret about what you have to write. Just do it. Finish your book of stories. Enantiodromia and Other Pine Mushrooms will be a fantastic book about the story of God, because it will be ground-breaking. It will open many eyes on human nature.

This is the gift you have to give, and the more you write the more you will be appreciated."

"I think that's enough stroking for one day. I know I asked for it, and you never refuse me; but I do get carried away. It's just my insecurity."

"That's what I'm here for. That's why so many people loved coming to me for confession; they felt safe with me. They felt that there was order and reason in the world when they walked out of the confessional. They came in confused and left with a sense that God was still in control of the world. That's what your writing does; it gives order to the world that feels so chaotic and confused. Your last book, The Pearl of Great Price is a magnificent jewel of order. It gives God his due, and I cannot tell you how much it is appreciated by our readers over here. It is a precious gem!"

"Thank you for that. I love it too. The look on Penny's face when she finished reading it was all I needed to know. Her face said, "I'm speechless.""

"That's how many readers are going to feel when they read it. It will leave them wondering why no one else has been able to piece the puzzle like you have. You connected the dots so well that you leave them speechless."

"That's the story of God, isn't it? That's the story of Everyman—and Noman! That's the story of life, which is the story of God. That's why Penny was speechless when she finished reading *The Pearl of Great Price*. There was nothing more to be said, was there. It told the story of God!"

"So you see, you have your own voice and need not worry. Now let your day unfold according to how the Spirit moves you."

"I will…"

19. Side Road or Main Road?

"Hi Padre. It's been a few weeks, but I'd like to ask you something. I don't know if I've been on a side road with my excursion into the world of the British television series *All Creatures Great and Small* which I began watching after I ran out of John Thaw's *Kavanagh QC* and *Inspector Morse* series (which also included *Inspector Lewis,* who was Morse's sergeant), but I felt strongly nudged to watch *All Creatures Great and Small* because they seemed to satisfy some need that I didn't know I had; a kind of historical need, possibly because of my past lifetimes in England. Was this the reason I watched these British weekly dramas?"

"You left a lot of unresolved issues with your lifetimes in the British Isles, and all of your issues are brought to the fore as you watch the TV dramas, which are doing you a lot of good. The stories touch your heart, which was not so open in your lifetimes in the British Isles. You had to acquaint yourself to the warm side of human nature in your fellow islanders, and these shows are doing the trick. Keep watching them until you no longer need to watch them. They are good for you."

"The people of the British Isles are an interesting lot. They seem to be a race apart from the continent, and this intrigues me. Is that the reason they can be so full of themselves and so idiosyncratic and eccentric?"

"Geography plays a big part in forming the national character, and island people are insulated from the continent and form their own identity. You've noticed this about Australians also, and New Zealanders; and you are correct in your observations of their national character. But the British people fascinate you most because of your lifetimes lived as a commoner and aristocrat. You've experienced both ends of the social spectrum, and you have a lot of both of those elements in your current personality. You can be very aristocratic about your common roots, and very common about your

aristocratic nature. You are an odd mixture of the high and low of the British character and this intrigues everyone who meets you."

"After watching all of these British dramas I've lost that hard edge I used to have for the British people. At one point in my life I called Britain a nation of eccentrics, perverts, and hypocrites; but I've softened my view considerably. I still think they're the most idiosyncratic and eccentric people in the world, but I'm not so sure about the pervert part. They exist everywhere. But watching all those British dramas has given me an insight into their national character, and I can understand why they are the way they are—because of their class system. It's both a blessing and a curse, and I guess I was seeing too much of the curse part which blinded me to the blessing part. Now I see both parts equally, and I find the British character both fascinating and amusing. I don't know how else to express it. They're just so full of themselves that I have to love and hate them at the same time. It's the enantiodromiac nature of their identity."

"Well said. That's why you felt compelled to watch all those British shows, because they rounded off your understanding of the human condition according to their national character. You healed yourself of your anger and resentment, and when your need to watch them stops you will be onto another side road."

"So it was a side road, then?"

"Every road is a side road of the main road of life, and it doesn't matter how far you walk down the side roads they all lead back to the main road. Yes; your little excursion into the world of British drama was a side road which you needed to explore. But as I said, it served your need and healed you of your deep seated anger and resentment. It was a good side road."

"It sounds like I don't need to explore this side road any further. I'm going to watch a few more episodes of *All Creatures Great and Small,* and I may even explore the actress Carol Drinkwater (who played James Harriot's wife Helen in over forty episodes before she was replaced by another actress for reasons which haven't been made quite clear), because of Carol Drinkwater's love for the olive tree. She has quite a story to tell, and I may order her Olive book series. They are memoirs of her love for her husband and the olive tree, both of which are related in a romantic way that seems to have made great material for writing. Her story fascinates me."

"For many reasons besides her romantic love and her love for the olive tree, but because of the way she affected you in her role as Helen in All Creatures Great and Small. She made an impression on you that stirred up your romantic nature, and you have a special fondness for her character; and because you know that an actor brings their life into the characters they play, you became fascinated by the life of Carol Drinkwater. And you were not wrong in your assessment: her character is one to be admired and respected. She stands heads and shoulders above the rest of the characters in that show, which is why you admire and respect her."

"And Siegfried also. His character on the show exemplifies the paradoxical nature of the British character, and I love how well he plays the part. It is sheer magic watching him play the double role of the paradoxical man; sheer magic!"

"He honed that part very well, and it will be the one he will be remembered for because he dares to let it all show—which the British are not wont to do. That's why you love him so. He dares to be the whole paradoxical man."

"Thank you for that. On to another subject. I've just completed a new spiritual musing. It's called "Gerbils of the Mind." Penny read it yesterday morning and loved it. She said that I am writing with a softer voice. Anyway, I've been nudged to write a musing that I've been putting off for a long time now; and I don't know what to do, because I know it's going to be demanding. The idea came to me a year or so ago, if not before, and it's about the world being perfect as it is. You know what I'm referring to, so I'm not going to explain because it would take up too much time and energy. Suffice to say that this is the way life is, and I'd like to write a musing on why it is the way it is and how we can reconcile ourselves to the reality of the never-ending process of man's becoming. I may call my musing "The Tumbler of Life.""

"Begin your musing with that thought in mind and see where it takes you. It is a big thought that needs to be put out there."

"And what about that other big thought that I'm afraid to write about? You know, the one about my impression of my spiritual community?"

"Work through that in your stories. They will see you through your uneasy feelings. Don't be afraid to write your stories as you

experienced them. Let them speak for themselves. That's what a good writer does. Don't judge. Just write your stories as you experienced them, and let the reader do the judging."

"I hear you. Thanks, Padre. Until next time…"

20. The Soul of the Aristocracy

Saturday, March 7, 2015

"I'd like to run a thought by you, if I may Padre. The last few days I've been watching the story of Winston Churchill's life, a man I've greatly admired and respected all of my life; but as I watched the eight part drama *Winston Churchill: The Wilderness Years* on You Tube starring Robert Hardy as Winston Churchill, who I thoroughly enjoy playing the role of Siegfried Farnon in *All Creatures Great and Small,* as well as Richard Burton's role as Winston Churchill in *The Gathering Storm*, and then an outstanding BBC semi-autobiography on Sir Winston Churchill, I began to see the aristocracy, into which Winston Churchill was born and bred, in a completely different light. It came to me in a sudden flash that the aristocracy is the inevitable product of human evolution in which the natural talents of man are given the opportunity to flourish and blossom; that's why the aristocratic are so sophisticated in mind, talent, and manners. And I have to confess, with this insight my instinctive antipathy for the aristocracy vanished.

"I was an aristocrat in British society in my immediate past lifetime, and I abhorred the "foul beast of honor and deceit" that the aristocracy represented; so I fled Britain and sailed to the new land of the Americas and became a fur trapper, which I've written about in my novel *Cathedral of My Past Lives*, and I carried my antipathy for the aristocracy into my current life. But after watching the story of Churchill's life my perspective shifted, and I saw the aristocracy for what it is: a natural product of social evolution in which the virtues of man are given an opportunity to flourish. True, one cannot dismiss the *enantiodromiac* factor of the shadow side of the aristocracy, which was what I despised in my past lifetime; but the virtue that I saw in Sir Winston Churchill's life was the result of his aristocratic breeding, and that's what shifted me out of my paradigm of anger and resentment for the British aristocracy. Winston Churchill could not have become the man who saved the British Empire and shut the gates of hell that Hitler had opened had he not been born and bred an aristocrat, because it was his natural inbred bearing that gave him the courage and talent and skill to stave off the dark forces that Hitler had unleashed to destroy man's free spirit. Sir Winston Churchill represented the soul of the aristocracy, and with his talent and creative genius that were bred into him by his aristocratic upbringing, he marshalled the British people to defend their way of life to their dying breath, and they beat off the forces of darkness that sought to destroy them. That's why I love and admire and respect Sir Winston Churchill. What do you think, Padre?"

"You are absolutely correct in your insight; the aristocracy is the rose flower of man's natural evolution, and it is the most beautiful flower in the garden of life. And in Sir Winston Churchill you have seen the blossom of man's natural talents in their most consummate expression. I too remember the speeches made by the Prime Minister of England, and they gave me great hope and courage. His words echoed throughout the world, and his words were as you say cultivated in the garden of his aristocratic culture. He was a man born to the mission of saving the world from the forces of evil, and he needed the best breeding to bring out the highest and most noble virtues of man; and that was the aristocracy, as you have correctly said. And this has healed another old wound for you."

"Yes, my anger and resentment for the aristocracy. I'm glad to have that weight off my shoulders. It was quite burdensome, Padre."

"Old wounds are very burdensome, specifically because we are not conscious of them. That's what makes life so interesting: we grow according to our need to heal, and the greater our need to heal, the more life we have to experience until we have realized enough consciousness to understand our wounds. As you watched all of those British dramas you grew in the consciousness you needed to understand the aristocracy's place and purpose in life, and in your understanding you healed yourself of your anger and resentment for the culture and sophistication of the well-bred aristocratic personality. What you were angry at was the shadow side of the aristocracy, which can be enough to drive the most patient and forgiving soul to distraction; but by seeing the virtues of the aristocracy you were free to accept the aristocratic personality as a

paradoxical whole, and that's the best that we can do with the life of man—to see it as a whole, and not one-sided."

"That must have been your dilemma every time you heard a confession, because you were exposed to the shadow side of life so often. How did you overcome that?"

"It was not easy. I saw life as black and white far too long before I outgrew this perspective. But over time I began to see that man was both black and white and that it was not possible to be whole and complete without God's help, which was what I was born to administer; and I listened and listened and forgave and forgave until one day I realized that man's nature is inherently double-sided. That's when I began to see that man was by nature a paradox, and that it was our purpose in life to make the two into one. That's when Christ's teaching finally made sense to me, and it was a glorious day when I made that discovery. That's why I enjoyed our talks when we worked on your book Healing with Padre Pio. I don't mind telling you that you are the first person who understood Jesus's teaching the way I had grown to understand it, and it was one of the most satisfying experiences of my life healing you of the vanity that kept you from transcending yourself."

"And I don't mind telling you that my experience with you as I worked on *Healing with Padre Pio* was also one of the most satisfying experiences of my life—if not *the* most satisfying. You brought everything together for me, and I could not have transcended myself without your help; so thank you, Padre."

"You're welcome, my friend..."

21. The Malignant Vanity Gene

Sunday, March 8, 2015

"And now the dreaded subject. I've been meaning to talk with you about this issue, but I've been putting it off because I dread the thought. However, when I read parts of my manuscript *The Summoning of Noman* this morning, I felt a sickening hollow every time I witnessed another example of my intrusive ego; and now I'm forced to open up the question of the malignant nature of my vanity. I'm not sure if malignant is the right word, but it's something very close; perhaps persistent self-love, or irreducible narcissism. I don't know, Padre; but I'd like to discuss this with you because it bothers me to read my work and see myself in that light. What can I do about it? I know I have a good book in *The Summoning of Noman*, but I can't help but feel that I'm too much in my own way. What do you say?"

"How can you not be? This book is after all the story of your parallel life, the life you returned to live to overcome the vanity of your first life. You cannot expect not to bump into yourself as you tell your story. With some judicious editing and gentle rewriting here and there, it will be one of your favorite books. Trust yourself to tell your story. When you trust yourself you connect with your Whole Self, and you will recognize what to edit out and what to retain. Don't fear humiliating yourself because you intrude in your own writing. That was your literary mentor's greatest fear. The biggest part of his writing was editing himself out of his stories, which wasn't easy for him to do as you noticed in his novel Across the River and Into the Trees. It was his worst book because his ego ruined it. But he made up for it with The Old Man and the Sea. So, you see; it's all about growth and understanding. With every book you write you grow a little more, and in your growth you evolve in your understanding. That's life."

"Is malignant vanity the right phrase? Do I have a malignant vanity gene, if I may express it this way? And if I do, did I inherit it from my family? I know I brought the vanity gene with me from some of my past lives, especially my lifetime in Paris, France; but I feel that my current family's history is equally responsible for my vanity gene. Am I being too creative here?"

"No, you are not. Vanity is both personal and familial. You chose your family because of the vanity in their line of history, and when your history mingled with their history you gave birth to what you call 'the malignant vanity gene.' It is not necessarily malignant, but very close; and had you not caught it in time, it would once again have destroyed your life—as it destroyed you former life."

"Do you mean my former past life, or my former parallel life?"

"In effect, both; but your former past life more so than your former current life because in your former current life you did not die so vain. You died disappointed in your life, and it was because of this disappointment that you chose to relive your life to achieve a different outcome. So your book The Summoning of Noman plays a significant role in your literary career, because it chronicles the history of coming to terms with your former current lifetime. This may sound confusing, but it's not. Just treat your former current life as another past life and it will all make sense. The only difference is that the memory of your former current life plays havoc with your dreams, because it keeps intruding into your mind. The only way to dispel this hold it has over you is to confront it once and for all. Let your dreams unfold on their own and let your unconscious work it out. It is infinitely wiser than you are because it has access to your Whole Self. In other words, don't fight yourself anymore."

"Alright, I'll do my best. I know that when I'm writing my spiritual musings I'm not so much in my own way, because I let my Muse take control of the creative process—as much as possible without losing control, that is. It's a two-way street, as you know; but it works in my musings. And it worked when I wrote *The Pearl of Great Price*. And speaking of *The Pearl*, I've been toying with the idea of writing a novella on Alice's funeral service. I have the strangest feeling that this story could turn out to be my entry into something I dread to write—my long relationship with my spiritual community. I honestly dread writing about it, even though I've tackled it in my book of stories (*Enantiodromia*); but I fear taking it on in one story alone, which is what I feel I'm being called to do."

"It will have to be done eventually, and since you have the context to do it justice why not write it now. It will be a great healing experience for you."

"I fear confronting the issue. I'm not sure how to go about it. I know I have to abandon to my Muse to do it justice, but the thought alone scares me."

"Don't be. Trust your Muse. Your Muse is neither for nor against anything. It is absolutely neutral and good. Your story will be your story, and it will be for the reader to judge it. That's the most you can do."

"Okay. But before I let you go, I have to at least rear the issue's ugly head just to begin the process: why do I fear facing my doubts about this teaching?"

"You have transcended your own voice and the voice of your spiritual community, and you see things differently now; that's why. You no longer need the crutch of the Inner Master as you did before, and that's your fear. You don't want to jeopardise the good of your teaching for what you now see. But what you now see is born of your own growth and understanding. It's neither good nor bad, it just is a new way of seeing. You now see the Inner Master as your Whole Self, and this changes the dynamic of your old teaching. Does this make sense now?"

"Yes; but I fear the dependency of the Inner Master is what causes so much shadow reality in my spiritual community, and that's what I'm afraid to write about because it will mean telling it as I now see it from my new perspective."

"Exactly. But just write your story and let it tell itself. Your perspective will be different from the way your community sees itself, but that's what good stories should do—offer a new perspective on life. Trust yourself. Trust your Muse. Trust the creative process to tell the story according to the reality of your own experiences; that's all you can do."

"And let the chips fall where they may…"

22. Waking Up Costs

Thursday, March 12, 2015

"Good morning, Padre. I was going to see if I could start another spiritual musing this morning, but for some reason I opened up this file to chat with you. Did you have something you wanted to talk about this morning?"

"I just want to let you know that I loved you spiritual musing on the movie Still Alice. That is an extraordinary insight that will bring comfort to a lot of people, because the fear of losing one's sense of self is much more prevalent than one could imagine. You connected the dots very nicely. Thank you."

"Why would you thank me?"

"Because you are helping to lighten the load, as it were. Humanity is burdened with much misunderstanding about its purpose in life, and with each spiritual musing that you write you help to lighten the load; and this lightens my load, because it's my chosen duty to help humanity find its way."

"Okay, I understand. We got the proof copy of *The Pearl of Great Price* yesterday, but I'm not happy with how it looks. It's nice to see the book in print, but I want to change the font size from 14 to 12, and I want to change the print to Times New Roman from Constantia because it will give the book a nicer look. Do you have any suggestions on how to improve the look and feel of the book? The story is all written, and all that remains is proofing the printed copy, so there's not much that can be said or added to the story; but about the look of the book, any ideas?"

"The aesthetic appeal is important to the reader. I would prefer the 12 font to give the book a tighter look. It compresses the words and makes the story more impactful; and I would also prefer Times New Roman also. Just go with your gut feeling and it will be what you want. I'm very happy with the story. It's a story that had to be told, because no-one has ever told this story before. It is unique."

"What happened yesterday, Padre? Those negative little forces came out of nowhere to throw me into a mild panic. Where did they come from?"

"You finished writing your spiritual musing yesterday, and it went out into the ethers; that's what stirred up the negative little forces, as you say. The conscious energy of your spiritual musing threatened the Archetypal Shadow, and it came back at you just to show you that it's still around. Don't worry. You have my protection and the protection of the Almighty with you at all times."

"I don't want to go there, but what about the Inner Master?"

"You always have the Inner Master's protection. He is with you every moment of your life. Just do not make the mistake of exteriorizing the Inner Master. That's what is causing so much contention in your spiritual community. The Inner Master is Divine Spirit, and until one realizes this they will always be subject to the influence of the Archetypal Shadow. You and the Inner Master are one, and that's the lesson that every soul must learn to realize their own divinity."

"So you think I should write my novella, then? The story about my relationship with my spiritual community?"

"As I said, it would make a wonderful story. A cautionary tale, if you will."

"I've brought this up before, more than once or twice; but I'm still inclined to bring it up again: why my fear of writing personal stories? I just don't want to go there, to that place where I am at my most personal; why?"

"You explained that in your prologue to The Pearl of Great Price. You fear getting burned by the energy of your private life by making it conscious for the reader in your stories. Your energy is very high, and as you write about your private life you have to re-experience your own energy; and this causes the burn that you fear to suffer. It is a spiritual burn. It will sear your soul of your attachment, and it is the letting go that scares you. You fear this kind of pain. I am familiar with this kind of pain, and it is the pain of self-awareness. Waking up costs."

"Don't I know it? Penny gave me a compliment when she read the last spiritual musing that I posted. She said it was like I was awake and everyone around me was asleep—in my musing, that is. My musing was called "What If…" But that seems to be the effect that my musings have, like the author is awake to how life works; and this affects the reader. Is that what stirred up the negative little forces yesterday? The conscious energy of my musing?"

"Exactly. Just keep on writing. There's not much the Archetypal Shadow can do to you, because you have gone way beyond the point of no return and you cannot be stopped in your mission. Just keep on writing. Trust yourself."

"I will. Thank you, Padre."

"You're more than welcome, my friend…"

23. Overcoming Antipathy

Saturday, March 14, 2015

"Do you remember what you said to me about a certain gentleman who had assembled too much information in his research on the historical Jesus and got confused and denied the existence of the man called Jesus of Nazareth?"

"Yes. We talked about this in our talks for your novel Healing with Padre Pio. I can see that you have outgrown your antipathy for the man."

"That's exactly what I was going to say. Ever since I read his books *The Pagan Christ* and *Water into Wine* I stopped bothering with Tom Harpur because I thought his passionate inquiry into the life of the historical Jesus was dead-ended, which I still do; but I came across his name on the web the other day and was nudged to look him up just to see what he was up to, and I see that he published a new book called *Born Again: My Journey from Fundamentalism to Freedom.* He still believes that the Jesus story is just a myth borrowed from antiquity, but something about his conviction in the non-existence of the historical Jesus affected me differently this time, and I actually saw the good in his perspective. It occurred to me as I listened to him talking on Moses Znaimer's *Ideas* that his belief that Jesus was a myth goes a long way to helping shift Christianity's perspective from God without to God within, if you know what I mean; because the essential theme of Harpur's belief is that we are all blessed with a spark of divine consciousness. For Tom Harpur, the Christ Consciousness lies within us all, and it's up to us to nurture it; and this is precisely my contention with Christianity also—as well as with my own spiritual community. The Inner Master is our Higher Self, and not the leader of my spiritual community; just as Harpur believes that the spark of divine consciousness is God within each and every person, and for Harpur it doesn't really matter if Jesus existed as a historical person or not, and I understood his point of view this time. And once I understood Harpur from my new and expanded perspective on life and the enantiodromiac nature of man, my antipathy for the man disappeared completely, and I admire him for his conviction. What do you think of that, Padre?"

"It's wonderful to drop that negative feeling. It frees you up to enjoy another man's journey to his true self. I can understand why you felt sorry for him as you listened to his talk, because you knew from your own journey where he has to go to find what he is looking for; but the fact that his conviction no longer bothers you says a great deal about your own growth. Wonderful!"

"Here's a question, then: will they ever be able to prove that Jesus of Nazareth existed as a real human being?"

"Yes. One day they will. New archeological finds will convince the world that a man called Jesus of Nazareth did walk the earth and did bring a teaching of salvation to mankind; but that won't be for a few years yet. It will be one of those serendipitous discoveries that will take the world by surprise."

"I was going to crack wise and ask you if Christianity would still be around when that happens, but I changed my mind because I know that it will be here till the end of this cycle of humanity; am I right or not?"

"Yes. It's here to stay until the next cycle of humanity, which won't be for a few thousand years or so. This should open up some new questions for you."

"Yes, it does. Life is a closed system, isn't it? It keeps looping back in on itself for the purpose of soul's growth and understanding, and it doesn't matter how long it takes—whether it be in this cycle of life, or the next—we are all going to keep coming back until we have outgrown the human condition; and then it's up to us whether we want to come back and help other souls to grow in their divinity. Am I correct in my understanding?"

"Pretty much so. This is a very wide perspective, and it's taken you a long time to expand your paradigm to view life this way; and I'm happy for you. And I'm happy that you continue to share your personal growth through writing. It will go a long way to helping other souls grow in their understanding of life."

"Padre, what was that dream I had last night all about? I dreamt that my three brothers were putting a cement roof on our family home. It was a strange dream, but it was as real as if it actually happened. What was that about?"

74

"Your family has grown in its concreteness, if you will. The consciousness of your family has become very rigid in its materialism. You family home symbolizes your family consciousness, and by cementing the roof of your family home your unconscious is telling you that you no longer reflect those material values; which should be a caution for you to not bring up the spiritual life with them."

"Are you talking about my books? Not to point them to my books, or my spiritual musings?"

"In effect, yes. They have chosen their path. Let them be, in your mind and in your life. You have transcended your family consciousness and you are beyond their understanding. Don't worry. The love is still there. Just not the understanding."

"And my niece? Should I continue our correspondence?"

"Your love for her is stronger than ever. Trust your heart to tell you what to do. It will always lead you in the right direction."

"I feel like I have gone too far with her by pointing her to my two novels, *Healing with Padre Pio* and *The Golden Seed*. Did I go too far?"

"No. You did it out of love for your niece. Just let it be and let God do the rest. You can do no more than follow your heart."

"I'm tempted to start another story based on Alice's funeral service, but I just don't seem to have the drive I used to have. I don't want to go there now, so I'm just going to wait and see what happens. If my Muse taps me on the shoulder one morning, I'll start the story. Otherwise I won't bother."

"Live, love, and enjoy your life. And since you get the most enjoyment out of writing, write and write and write and just let it happen."

"Thanks Padre. I can always count on you to assuage my feelings of anxiety. I'd sure like to write that story, though. It would do me wonders."

"It would, and it will. Trust yourself to let it happen and it will."

"Good. I will. Until next time, then…"

24. Getting Permission from My Muse

"I've done several more edits of my book *The Pearl of Great Price,* and as of yesterday I was ninety-nine percent happy with it. I'm going to read it one more time before I turn it over to Penny and I hope I'm as happy still. I don't know what else I can do to improve it; but I do know it's not like any story anyone has ever written, because it's so unique. Tell me, Padre; in all honesty, what do you think of it?"

"The Pearl of Great Price is incomparable. It is so full of wisdom that one would be hard-pressed to find one single book with so many answers. You should be proud of your story. It is a story that will find its way to all the right people. And yes, follow your gut and send it to all those people you have thought of sending it to; not only will they appreciate it, but they will help launch your career."

"I don't want to repeat myself, but I'm back to that place where I want to feel sorry for myself. I know what I have to do, but I can't seem to do it. I drew up a tentative graph for my new novel (which I have called "my big novel"), but that's as far as I got. My working title is "The Funeral Service," and it will use Alice's funeral service as the connecting principle—the hub of the wheel, as it were. I don't know what to make of it, but I feel that once I get into it I may have to dig deep into myself for the stories that I fear writing about, and by stories I mean my relationship with my spiritual community. I don't want to go there, but I fear I have to."

"Why don't you read some spiritual biographies, like St. Teresa of Avila's story? It may surprise you. You will learn about the inside of her cloistered experience. I could tell you about my life, but that's another story. You're familiar enough with my private life to understand the ins and outs of the cloistered life, but you have to read about the cloistered life from the cloistered; that's the only way you can get an inside look at the private and secret life of the members. You want to write about the unseen part of your initiate's life as a member of your spiritual community; then do it. That's the only way

the story will ever be told. Who else has the objectivity to do it justice? As you say, you can see both sides now."

"Do you mind if I open a file right now and catch the first few lines? I'd like to see if my Muse is really serious about this story."

"By all means..."

"Okay, I opened up a new file and got the title for my first chapter, which I've called "A Lack of Grace." And I began the chapter with a short piece of dialogue; but I don't know where it's going to go from there. Is that a good entry point into my story? I want it to be my big novel, and I have to be expansive in the expression of my emotions; but I'm going to need your help on this one, Padre. I don't think I can go there on my own. I have to, of course; but you know what I mean."

"I know exactly what you mean. And yes, it is an excellent entry point for your BIG NOVEL. *I stress this because it will demand the most of you; but do not fear, because you have been preparing for this story for a long time. It will give you the opportunity to tell it as it was, to borrow your literary mentor's words* (Hemingway), *and the more you tell it as it was, the easier it will come; that's the law of creative expression.* TRUST YOURSELF. *You've made a good start, now just work on it a little bit each day. And you're right to read Alice Munroe's stories. They will give you the right kind of feeling to be expansive in your emotional expression. She is a master of the short story, and each chapter of your novel will be like a short story; but all of your stories will be connected by the central theme of your story— the funeral service, which brings all the stories home to the central feelings that you have to get out of your system about your spiritual community. Just do it."*

"Thank you for the encouragement. I need it."

"That's what I'm here for. I believe in you, my friend. I only wish that you would believe in yourself as much as I believe in you, and Penny. She has a lot of faith in your writing. How else could she devote so much time to it?"

"I know. And I'm more grateful than I can express, because without her my books would all be piled up in boxes somewhere—if they were written at all, that is; because without Penny's support I wouldn't be free to write."

"You have the freedom and the time, and once you get into your new novel it will get hold of you and you won't be able to stop yourself. You Muse is waiting to grab your attention. All you have to do is give it permission."

"Give my Muse permission? That's a new one. What does that mean? Isn't my Muse the one who gives me permission, as it were?"

"That's a complicated question. Your Muse is your Higher Self, as you very well know; but your Higher Self cannot operate without your permission, whether your permission is implicit or explicit. More often than not, a writer's permission is implicit, and one's Muse will empower them with the gift of their talent; but without permission the writer operates on mind energy alone, and emotional energy; but that is not enough to make a good story. A writer needs the gift of his Muse, which is the gift of one's Higher Self that is one with the Whole. And the Whole will express itself according to one's life, which makes a story a very personal expression. This is what it means to write with your own voice. A writer's voice is the voice of his whole self, which speaks for the Whole in an individual way. So, why don't you formally invite your Muse to grant you the gift of expressing yourself from your whole self? That'll save you a lot of heartache."

"I will. Give me a moment to compose myself."

"Granted..."

"I hereby call upon my Muse to grant me the gift of my talent, that I may give expression to the whole of me in my new novel *The Funeral Service* and all of my other writing. Here is what I request of you: 1. the clarity and elegance of an Alice Munroe story; 2. the depth and wisdom of Carl Gustav Jung; 3. the humility and compassion of St. Padre Pio; love and honesty of the mystic poet Rumi; the gift of expressive prose like John Updike; and the erudition of all my knowledge, in the manner of Professor Harold Bloom. If you can grant me these gifts, I'd be eternally grateful. Thank you."

"Granted. Now go about your work, and remember: TRUST YOURSELF. Have a wonderful day, my friend..."

25. The Niqab Controversy

Saturday, March 28, 2015

"I wrote a new spiritual musing called "A Tempest in a Teapot," inspired by a Muslim woman from Mississauga, Ontario who refused to take off her niqab (face covering) for her oath-taking ceremony for her Canadian citizenship; and, in all honesty Padre, I had no idea that this musing was the second half of the spiritual musing I wrote several weeks earlier, "To Be and Not to Be, Personal Identity and Alzheimer's." It completed the thought on personal identity, and I'm very grateful to my Muse for sparking the idea. And I have to share this with you. After I wrote "A Tempest in a Teapot," I felt that for the first time in my writing I stood above the polar opposites of life, in that place that Joni Mitchell's song "Both Sides Now" alludes to but doesn't quite understand, the only difference being that I understand, which is why I wrote my spiritual musing on the niqab controversy."

"It completed the thought beautifully. This is what it means by going with life and the living. You took a life-situation and dealt with it creatively. That's what Jesus means in Glenda Green's book, and you are good at doing this because you get your best ideas from life; so keep it up. Soon, very soon, you will be given another idea for a spiritual musing; and it will come from a life-situation also."

"I get the feeling that this is leading somewhere, to a greater thought; quite possible to that place of understanding what it means to live a karma-free life, as you indicated to me in one of my spiritual healing sessions. I think I'm approaching that place of understanding, which seems to me to be a natural extension of the evolution of our individual identity through life, to that place of transcendence where one KNOWS, and chooses to live his life karma free. Am I close?"

"You've got it, but you have to experience it more and more to be fully realized in the experience of your own KNOWING. It is a big breakthrough, and you will continue to break more and more ground as you follow life and the living; meaning, as you ground yourself more in the NOW."

"I'm sorry to say, I don't feel that inspiration that fires up my novel writing; that's why I'm not working on my new novel "The Funeral Service." For some reason, I'm avoiding it. But then, I did break off to write my musing "A Tempest in a Teapot," which took considerable research and weaving to create the dialectical thought on the whole niqab issue; so I didn't have much creative energy left over for novel writing. I don't know it that's an excuse, or a justifiable reason."

"Both. But in this case, acceptable; so don't fret. You do only have so much creative energy for each day, and when you exhaust your allotted amount you have little left for new thought. That's why you don't feel like doing anything after you have a good morning of writing. But you can supplement your energies by going out for walks and taking care of yourself a little better, and not watching so much TV and getting more sleep. But that's up to you, isn't it?"

"Of course it is, and I have to fight myself from guilt-tripping myself, and that in itself uses up a lot of my energy!"

"Well said. You know what this means, then; don't you?"

"Of course. It means that I have to resolve this inner conflict, because once resolved the leak in my energy field will be sealed and I will have more energy to do what I want to do but won't allow myself to do; right?"

"Right. And how do you propose to resolve your conflict?"

"I'd prefer that you tell me."

"DO, DO, and DO! The more you DO, the more energy you will have to DO; and the more energy you have to DO, the less conflicted you will be. Capisce?"

"Yes, I understand…"

26. Regaining My Sense of Purpose

Wednesday, April 1, 2015

"I don't know where to begin, but I have to begin somewhere because I have to get to the bottom of my situation. I don't want to call it a depression, but I think that's what it is. I've been slowly taken over by a profound sense of futility, as though whatever I do has no relevance, and this eats away my sense of meaning and purpose. If this isn't depression, I don't know what is. So, last night before I went to bed I took out my Wordsworth and read two of his best poems to pick up my spirit; "Resolution and Independence," and the "Character of the Happy Warrior." And this morning as I waited for the coffee to drip I read them both again. Now I am opening up a dialogue with you because I can't go on this way. Life-fatigue has got me in its grip, and it's squeezing the spirit out of me. I have much more to say, but please offer me some hope that I may regain my sense of purpose…"

"The life of a writer is never easy, no matter how successful the writer, because the writer is always working with the creative energies of life and they can turn one's life upside down before one knows it. This is the nature of the creative current, to keep one's life always on the move, always on the hunt for more and more meaning; and it seems that you have poured yourself into your last book and feel empty of meaning and the doldrums have set in. The Pearl of Great Price is a very powerful book, taking the most and best that you had to give; and to be quite honest, I'm surprised that you are even this healthy given what you gave to your book. You need to replenish yourself, and reading poetry is a good way to start. Read those two poems out loud every morning and every evening before you go to bed; they will set up your vibrations for the day. You have to tone yourself to the higher energies of the creative current, and reading those poems are a good way to start."

"But it's more than that, isn't it?"

"It always is, but there is only so much we can know for our necessary purpose; and you need not know more to get you back on track."

"Here's a question for you, then: why do I feel like I'm wasting my time when I read something that is not directly related to the central theme of my life—the Way? Why cannot I simply enjoy reading a short story? I know the value of a short story, because I'm only too familiar with the aesthetic purpose of the story—which is to carry the meaning of the life experience, or the inherent purpose of the human condition as expressed in the story; but why do I avoid it? What is this fear of wasting my time? I feel I'm always sucked into a bog of NOT-DOING just to keep me from DOING. Is there a conflict in my soul? Are the demons of NOT-DOING out to get me and destroy my life?"

"In many ways, yes. This is what life is all about, to keep you trapped in the vast and endless cycle of NON-BEING, that state of consciousness that is neither one nor the other where you waste your life away doing the least amount possible until you get overwhelmed by your own irrelevance."

"Is that why people kill themselves?"

"In many cases, yes."

"I don't doubt it, the way I felt yesterday. So, there seems to be a process by which this life-denying consciousness takes over one's mind; a process that I see as the slow disintegration of one's sense of worth. The more one let's oneself go, the less attention one pays to the details of his life, the more life-denying energy he creates to nourish the demon of his non-being; and when the demon is feeling hungry, he tempts one to do less, and less, and less. And next thing you know, one is in such a state that he doesn't want to do anything and sinks into depression. How close to the mark am I in my observation?"

"There is much more truth to what you say than you realize. But you have the gist of the depressive spiral, and the solution is to DO. As you say, you have to start paying attention to the details of your life—your hygiene, your clothes should be fresh and clean, and develop stricter eating habits so you don't indulge yourself at every whim. To get your life back on track you have to be clever, and resourceful. You were always clever and resourceful. Call back those skills and put them to good use. You need them to get your life back in working order."

"Let's hope I can…"

27. Going Back to My Spiritual Healing

Friday, April 3, 2015

"I just finished reading my last spiritual healing session with you in my novel *Healing with Padre Pio*, and I feel good because being with you in my session again lifted up my spirits; that's why I'd like to chat with you now. I think in all sincerity that I'm ready for our next project together. What do you say we try to get to it this summer? I'd love the challenge of another book with you."

"It will happen when it happens. You have done much to prepare yourself for our next project together, and I promise that it will happen—in this lifetime. It may happen this summer. The choice is yours to make."

"Would you like to see it happen this summer?"

"I would love to see it happen anytime, because whenever it happens it will prove to be very rewarding for both of us, and for our psychic medium."

"Here's a thought I'd like to run by you now, which I know we will explore much deeper when we get together through our psychic medium: when all is said and done about spiritual paths and all this new knowledge about other worlds and parallel lives and all of that, it all comes back to the journey of the self through vanity to humility; am I correct in my observation, as I am making clear with every spiritual musing that I am writing? That it's all about growth and understanding, as you put it in one of our sessions? And all of this fuss is nothing but an exciting distraction from the responsibility of our individual journey?"

You have hit the nail on the head, as they say. Yes, it all comes back to the individual self and how one lives his/her life. It's all a glorious distraction to keep the self away from doing what it was born to do, which is to take account of its life and live it responsibly and not selfishly. This is the central problem that the world has to contend with today, the selfish indulgence of carnal pleasures. Not in a sinful way, as such; but in a vast and all-consuming way that distracts one from the spiritual life, which is what we're born to learn about and realize. Just keep writing your spiritual musings, because you offer a thoughtful perspective that forces people to look at life more responsibly. Your musings are getting better and better. They have broken through to a new level, and it will pay off for you."

"Can I ask a personal favor?"

"By all means."

"I know it's against protocol, but I need a boost of energy; and I don't want to get it from a life shock, because that could kill me. I'd like a boost of graceful nature, one which will lift my spirits to a better place, because in all honest I just don't seem to have it in me to re-ignite my life. I'm just plodding along, doing my daily writing; and I don't have the will power to re-ignite my life. So if at all possible, could I get a graceful boost to get me started? Now that I've asked, I feel shame for asking; and I'd like to rethink my request..."

"No need. Your request is duly noted, and I have already begun the transfer of energy from you own account. You need not worry about payment, as it is your own energy that you will be drawing upon; so no need for shame. Your account can handle it, and so much more. Keep your eyes and ears open the next few days, because you will be in a position to receive what you have requested, and it will come to you when you least expect. By all means, I am glad you asked."

"Okay. Here's why I asked. I want to slim down, read poetry again, do some nice spontaneous things with Penny, get our life back on track, and write with that fervor that I used to have. That's why I asked. And I'd like our triplex to sell this summer so Penny and I can get a life."

"Request granted, and all drawn from your own account."

"Can you explain what you mean by this?"

"You have made many deposits in your karmic account, and you have seldom drawn upon it; only when you had to. You have never drawn from your account voluntarily as you are requesting now; and your request has been granted."

"One more thing, right now: please cast that demon fear out of my mind. It has just lodged itself there, and I want it out. Please?"

"Done. Your life is yours. Live, love, and enjoy your life."

"Thank you."

"You're welcome, my good friend."

"I can't wait to see you in person, Padre; but that will happen when it happens. For now, I think I have a few more books to put out."

"You do. And do what you plan to do with The Pearl of Great Price. Send a copy to those people you planned to send a copy to. They will not only appreciate it, but will help you launch the book and your career. I promise!"

"Okay. Thank you. *Ciao* for now..."

28. Too Excited to Write

Friday, April 10, 2015

"Padre, I'm too excited to write; I mean, work on my new book that I was called by my Muse the other day to write—*Gurdjieff Was Wrong, But His Teaching Works*. I wrote the first two and a half pages the day I was called, but I stopped working on it the day after (which was yesterday) because I was out of sorts because of something that I did that I am not proud of; but this morning I was nudged to read the last chapter of Gurdjieff's book *Life Is Real Only Then, When I Am*, and I was so excited by Gurdjieff's coincidence in that chapter because it addressed the theme of desperation and synchronicity in the first chapter of my new book *Gurdjieff Was Wrong, But His Teaching Works* that I am too excited to write now, especially since Gurdjieff's coincidence came after I read to Penny over coffee this morning Wordsworth's poem "Resolution and Independence" in which Wordsworth relates the extraordinary coincidence of meeting the leech gatherer on the lonely moor who picked up his dejected spirits—a providential gift! That's what coincidences and synchronicities are—a divine grace granted by God! That's why I'm too excited to work on my chapter this morning. I have to settle down first. Which I'm doing with my active imagination exercise of talking with you—"

"First things first. Don't fret about the other night. You were burdened with a lot of excess negative energy that had to be dispelled, you dispelled it quickly but to your moral discomfort; but that's alright. No harm done. Now, you did get your call as I expected, and you are inspired to write your story; which is exactly what you requested—to re-ignite your life. Gurdjieff was a big influence—the biggest influence on your life, and this new book will be your thanks and appreciation for all he did for you. Write it from your heart and pour everything you have into it, because it is the perfect medium to tell your story. This is your chance to set the record straight on many, many things. You are quite right to be annoyed with the conclusions

the world has come to about the soul of man, and you have to set the record straight with your story. So do it without qualms. And I can promise you, the more you devote yourself to your new book, the more focussed your attention will be and the more you will transcend yourself and center yourself in the place that you want to be—the ideal place for your optimum comfort, physical, emotional, mental, spiritual, and economical! I promise you, my friend; because once you step into this mission, you step into the sacred mission of lifting up the consciousness of life, and when one when steps into that mission he is granted special favors. Wait and see."

"Given what you told me in our last chat and how I was re-ignited by the call to write my new book *Gurdjieff Was Wrong, But His Teaching Works*—which, incidentally, came to me when I least expected, just like you said!—I have to believe what you are telling me now; and I can't wait to see! So I'm going to try to settle down first, and maybe later I will work on my chapter. I think I'm going to shower and wash my hair, and then make some breakfast—I have a yen for a couple of boiled eggs; and then I may work on my book. So, thank you Padre. What you promised came true, and that's always a good feeling."

"You're welcome. Go and live your day and let the creative juices settle down and then you can write with dispassionate passion, which will give your insights greater clarity. Enjoy your day."

"Thank you, Padre; until we chat again…"

29. Still Reading Gurdjieff Material

Sunday, April 12, 2015

"For the past two days I've been re-reading some of my Gurdjieff books, starting with *Gurdjieff Remembered*, by Fritz Peters, and now I'm into *The Unknowable Gurdjieff*, by Margaret Anderson, plus all of my reading online, especially interviews with William Patrick Patterson, author of *Georgi Ivanovitch Gurdjieff: The Man, The Teaching, His Mission*, as well as other material from *The Gurdjieff Journal* web site, plus other stuff, and all because I want to saturate myself with the Gurdjieff Work and awaken old memories of my years living "the way of the sly man," which was Gurdjieff's term for the secret teaching of the Work; but I'm almost ready to get back to my own story that I started writing last week, the strange story of how I "squared the circle" with Gurdjieff's teaching. I had to stop writing my story because I was too excited when I read Gurdjieff's book *Life Is Real Only Then, When I Am*, because of the remarkable coincidence that Gurdjieff reveals at the end of his book in the chapter "The Outer and Inner World of Man," because his coincidence was coincidental to my story! What do you think of that? It's like the creative unconscious knows all and brings everything to the singularity of the Now Moment. Any thoughts, Padre?"

"Yes, plenty. This is the aim of your book, to bring your story to the Now Moment, the ever-present reality of one's life; which is why your Muse, if we can call it that for simplicity's sake (as you say, your creative unconscious for the sake of the overall telling), chose the entry point that it did so you can always have the Now Moment to come back to in the telling. I think it would not be far-fetched to say that this could very well be your magnum opus. It all depends upon how much you want to reveal. But, knowing you, you will let your Muse decide."

"All of the reading I've done so far has done nothing more than confirm my feeling that I HAVE to tell my story of "squaring the circle," because it will bring spiritual clarity to the question of man's purpose in life, which I'm happy to say was confirmed by you in my novel *Healing with Padre Pio*. I never expected this novel to have as much meaning as it does; it just seems to be revealing more and more every time I reflect on my journey to my true self. It brought me to you, the person that I had arranged to work with when I came back to live my life over again; or did I get that wrong. Did we make arrangements before I came back into my life, or while I was in my life?"

"Before and after. We worked together before in other lifetimes as well, but this you will learn about when we do your other book with the medium. For now concentrate your best energies on your Gurdjieff book. This book is necessary, and I mean NECESSARY, because it will break a mold that needs breaking. Yes, you are correct to call yourself a "bubble burster," because this is what you do; and now you are going to burst one of the biggest bubbles of all in the tradition of esoteric literature. This is why you were called to write your story."

"Can I expect your guidance in my writing?"

"Of course. I'm happy to assist you in your process."

"At the risk—no risk involved; any advice you can give me?"

"Your book will find its own way. Trust your instincts. Listen to the little voices when they speak to you. They will come in many ways. They will be from everyone who would like to see your book written. Yes, Carl Jung also. He is adamant that you write your story. It will be your Red Book. That's what he told me to tell you. Just don't be afraid to tell it. Advice? Make a habit of working on your book every morning—before reading or anything else. This must be your FIRST obligation every morning, because it is too easy to be distracted. This is your first obligation. Everything else comes second, and after your day's writing. I say this because you MUST develop the habit of getting into the ZONE of your book, that special atmosphere, or consciousness of your story; and once you have established a firm connection, your story will flow effortlessly and with abundant recollection of your life in the Work. I have all the confidence in you."

"You certainly are my confidence booster. I guess what I really want is to establish an unfettered connection with my creative unconscious, a direct link-up, if this is possible. Is it?"

"Yes, it is; and you will come very, very close. Close enough to get your story written and boost your moral on the mystical connection. Yes, I have that connection directly, as you assume; but I didn't make it completely until I crossed over. You will come close, as I said; but I cannot say any more for now. Just write, and work on your story every day. Yes, you may and will write your spiritual musings to keep your blog fresh, and they will draw their own readers. Your recent musings have caused quite the stir in the minds of the reader. They can't quite place you. You don't seem to fit into anyone's box, and that puzzles them. Good."

"Okay; thank you, Padre."

"You're welcome…"

30. Let's Talk

Monday, April 27, 2015

"I'd like to talk, if I may Padre. It's not pressing, but I have to talk to you just to ease the tension. I started my book *Gurdjieff Was Wrong, But His Teaching Works,* and I'm getting into the flow of the story; but something is happening to me, as though the story is offering me a new perspective, and to be quite honest I don't know how I feel about this. I feel unsettled, like my memories are being tossed like a salad, and I don't know how to deal with this feeling. Whenever I begin working on my book, I think it's going to go one way; but then the book finds its own direction, and though I like where it takes me it leaves me unsettled. Why?"

"This is your reason for writing it, to organize your thoughts and feelings and come to a complete understanding of your Gurdjieff experience. Already you have changed how you feel about Gurdjieff, knowing what you do from what you have written. You have a much clearer perspective now that you have organized your thoughts and feelings. You no longer have that hero worship that you had while living his teaching. The good thing is that you never throw out the baby with the bath water, which is a very commendable trait; but to see the dirty bathwater was a problem that you had all of your life. Now you are pouring in new and clean water into the tub and the baby can be cleansed properly as the old dirty bathwater is washed down the drain; the new bathwater in this case being your understanding of Gurdjieff's teaching, which is that man is born with an immortal soul and does not die "merde" as Gurdjieff believed."

"I have to ask, Padre; I know he believed that man is not born with an immoral soul, but did he get this belief from the ancient esoteric traditions of the East? Those hidden schools that taught how to create one's own soul? He called his teaching 'esoteric Christianity,' and I know we talked about this in my novel *Healing with Padre Pio,* but I'm still not quite clear on this. Was this all a misperception of how soul evolves through life, as I have intuited?

And by this I mean that soul is both being and non-being, and these esoteric schools taught one how to, as Jesus would say, 'make the two into one'? Is this the core issue of this whole confusion?"

"You have intuited correctly. And when you explain this in your book you will put a lot of minds to ease. So by all means, just continue working on your story. And yes, it is me who keeps insisting 'WRITE YOUR STORY.'"

"It's costing me, Padre."

"I know. But you have no choice, do you? This is what you have lived for, to explain the mystery of your becoming. You have memories of all the things that you have done in your life that have embarrassed and humiliated you; but, as I told you before, you needed these experiences to get to where you are today. So ask yourself, are you happy with what you have achieved?"

"All in all, yes; I'm very happy."

"Then keep this thought in mind when those memories come to disturb you. They will dwindle as you write your story, because once they have been brought into the light of your conscious mind they will cease to have power over you. Just write them out of your system. That is the cure that all writers use to heal themselves of the mortal wounds of their own unhappy memories."

"I seem to have so many, though."

"Yes, because you had to work your way through the consciousness of non-being; not only your own non-being, but the non-being of Everyman. That's the chapter you're working on now, and it will be very powerful when you complete it. You have a few pages to go yet before it is finished. Don't rush it. Work into it as you will. It will come on its own, and I am here to guide you."

"Okay, here's a question then: how could a man as evolved as George Ivanovich Gurdjieff get it so wrong?"

"But did he? As your title says, his teaching works; and why does it work if he got it so wrong? He got the teaching right, but as you said his premise was wrong; and that's what your book is going to show."

"But look at the damage his teaching has left in its wake."

"It is and it isn't damage. This is the experience that these souls need. All teachings lead to the self, and Gurdjieff's teaching speeds up the process; that's all. The unfortunate part is that his

teaching leaves them at the edge of the mystery, and this they will have to learn on another path once they get over what they have learned from Gurdjieff's teaching. It takes time. But time is forever. This is the deep mystery that you are approaching, the NOW *of* ETERNITY.*"*

"Padre, would you please cast out my demon fears. I can't stand the apprehension any longer—"

"Rest easy, my friend; your fears are imaginary."

"Thank you. What did you think of my last spiritual musing that I posted on my blog, 'The Shadow Personality'?"

"Very informative. It opened a lot of eyes. I enjoyed it very much. You have arrived at an understanding of life that brings clarity to the human condition, and this intimidates your friends and readers. Don't fret. Just keep doing what you are doing and don't worry about the feedback. Your readers respect you but are intimidated by your writing. Just keep writing and let the world unfold on its own. Your contribution will be acknowledged one day, and you will be around to see it; I promise you. And I do not say this lightly."

"And now about the discipline? I'm going to write a new spiritual musing that I was called upon yesterday to write. My title is going to be 'Weak Discipline.' You know where I'm going with this. Am I ever going to get back some of my 'strong' discipline; because this is what I would love to get back to. I NEED it!"

"Make it happen and it will be yours. That's all I can say. You are the author of your own life. Write it into your script."

"If only it were that easy!"

"But it is that easy. I also went through many days and weeks and months of tortured doubt in my own discipline, and I prayed and prayed and prayed with no results. And then my fears went away one day and I was into the mode of living that I had hoped to be in, and it all came about without asking. It just happened as I did what I was supposed to do to make it happen. The DOING *is what counts. In the* DOING *comes the reality. Just write strong discipline into your script and start the process, inch by inch and not mile by mile. To run the mile you have to run the inch first. That's your starting point. Inch by inch."*

"Nice image. You are fantastic at creating the right image for the concept that I want to make clear. Inch by inch it is, then; and I will write my musing to get the process started. I'll try to write the musing today. Thank you for this, Padre."

"*You're welcome…*"

31. Life Is an Individual Maze

Wednesday, May 6, 2015

"Before I get to the thought that I want to discuss with you, I have to tell you that I wrote a surprising little spiritual musing yesterday. It's titled, "It's All about Balance," and it speaks to the issue of how religions, philosophies, and other paths function like the training wheels that children use when they learn how to ride a bicycle; and when they have learned how to balance themselves, they no longer need the training wheels. My musing was about how I outgrew my training wheels. What do you think of my musing?"

"Excellent metaphor. You have revealed the essential purpose of all spiritual paths, which is to make one learn to become a law unto oneself. You have come a long way, my friend. Now, what thought would you like to talk about today?"

"I'm not up to working on my book today, perhaps because I exhausted myself creatively yesterday with my spiritual musing, I don't know; but I got my Sunday *Star* yesterday and sat on the front deck and read both Saturday's two papers, the *Globe and Mail*, and the *National Post*, and Sunday's *Toronto Star*, and I got confirmation on the idea for a spiritual musing that I was called to write several weeks ago, a musing titled "Why Be Good?" but I'm not up to writing it yet; and this morning I went online and checked out some new books on Gurdjieff just to avoid working on my book, but the thought came to me from all my newspaper reading yesterday and my perusal of the books on Amazon that life is a maze that everyone is born into and the purpose of life is to work one's way out. Actually, our life is an individual maze within the maze of life; which makes life such a puzzle. That's the impression that came to me as I perused all those new books on Gurdjieff by students of his teaching, because all they did for me was confirm their own maze and how they were trying to find their way out; and it depressed me, actually. Is that why you keep insisting, WRITE YOUR OWN STORY?"

"That's precisely why I keep insisting that you write your own story. You have found your way out of your own maze, and the maze

of life; this is why your story is so original. All the reading you do helps to expand your knowledge of the maze that other people have to work their way through, but they don't add to your life in terms of new knowledge as such; they just satisfy your curiosity about how other people work their way out, and that can be depressing because most get stuck in their own maze and in the maze of life. Doubly depressing if they are stuck in both. So just write your own story and get it out there."

"I have a feeling this one's going to be a big book, though. I think maybe four hundred pages. I'm on page forty-five so far, and it seems to have a mind of its own despite the fact that it's my personal story."

"That's good. Your creative unconscious is organizing your life in a way that will make the most literary and aesthetic sense. Enjoy the experience. It is going to be a very, very rewarding book; in more ways than one."

"So, what do you think of this maze concept?"

"Life is a maze, both personally and universally; and it takes a long time to even realize that we are born into a maze, and even longer to find our way out. That's why your new book is so important. It is the story of how you found your way out of your personal maze and the maze of life."

"Okay, not the concept of monumental philosophical edifices, like the Gurdjieff doctrine of salvation. He never called it a doctrine of salvation, but that's how I'm beginning to see it now; and, in all honesty, I'm not happy about what I see, because it has become no less of a maze than any other teaching that keeps one trapped in a perspective that is so puzzling. Gurdjieff's teaching works, but good God one has to really work on oneself to find one's way out. I did, and I can speak to the experience; but what about all those students who got lost in the doctrine? How depressing it must be to be lost in a teaching that you can't find your way out of; it's hard for me to even think about it."

"Yes, it is; but that's life. Life's purpose is to create conditions for soul to grow in understanding, and the more difficult the conditions are the more opportunity soul has to grow in understanding. It's all good, my friend."

"Yes, I see both sides of life now, thank goodness; but when I focus too much on the negative, it sure can get depressing."

"I know. I spent a lot of time focusing on the depressing in my lifetime as a Capuchin priest. Every time I heard confessions I was sent into that state which I did not want to call depression, but it was; and I prayed, and prayed. That's how I dealt with my depression."

"Everybody wants a magic formula for life; a formula for love, health, wealth, and happiness. Everybody wants a formula. That's what drives people to buy into so many things—new teachings, new products, new relationships. It's all about finding the right formula; isn't it?"

"I couldn't have expressed it better. Yes, it's all about finding the right formula, because man does not want to accept the responsibility that he is the author of his own fate. Life is about accepting responsibility for our own life, this is why I enjoyed your musing "It's All about Balance." It says it all."

"I may just be ready to write my musing Why Be Good? I may start it; I don't know if I can finish it. I'll see."

"Since you're not up to working on your book, try your hand on this musing; it may prove to be more than you think. I like the title very much."

"Okay, Padre; with your blessing, I'm going to start it. Thanks for chatting with me this morning."

"You're welcome, my friend..."

32. Both Sides of Life

Thursday, May 7, 2015

"Good morning, Padre. I just finished writing—editing, actually; I finished writing it yesterday morning—a new spiritual musing called "The Mystery behind Joni Mitchell's Song "Both Sides Now," and I'm more than thrilled with how it turned out. It surprised me, because it found its own way into insights I didn't expect. But that's the nature of the creative process, isn't it? After all, this is precisely why I write my spiritual musings; to explore new spiritual horizons."

"This has to be one of your finest pieces of writing. You have excelled yourself with this musing. It will open doors for you. Trust the giver."

"What do you mean by that? Trust the giver?"

"You know the principle: you receive what you give. What you have given in this spiritual musing is the key to the mystery of the human condition, and the more discerning reader will see it. Your musing will be subject to much study. Joni Mitchell will contact you. Be sure of it."

"How will she hear of my musing?"

"It will find its way to her. It is destined."

"I knew that I would write a musing on her song "Both Sides Now," but it was slow going for a while. Once it found its way, after two day's research online, it opened up and showed me a picture that offers a wonderful glimpse at how life works; this is why I'm more than thrilled how it turned out. It's all about trusting the creative process, isn't it? I know I'm putting off working on my new book on my life with Gurdjieff, but I was called to write my three new spiritual musings. I guess I have to put my nose to the grindstone now and work on my book."

"The break did you good. This way when you go back you'll have a fresh perspective. Your book is very, very personal; and you have to distance yourself to be so objectively personal. It's not

unheard of for writers to break off and do other writing when they are working on a big book. It's a process, and if it works for you just keep doing it."

"I know it's working for me, because my reading during the day has opened me up to the perspective that I want to expand upon in my Gurdjieff book—the perspective that explains his philosophical imperative to bring his students to the edge of life so they can awaken to their mortality; a perspective that is so frightening that it scared the wits out of many followers. That has to be seen for what it is, and that's what I've been gestating in my unconscious. I'm not quite ready yet to work it out in my book, but I'm getting there. I guess I'm hesitating because it brings Christ's teaching into the picture. Is that why I'm hesitating?"

"It is a big principle, and you have to be completely confident in your perspective; that's why you are reading the books you are. You have to firm up your conviction, which I personally see needs no confirmation. But you're the writer, and you have to follow your own creative instincts."

"I have to tell you, Padre; I've been reading through Glenda Green's books again (*The Keys of Jeshua,* and *Love without End*), and I love the way Jesus comes through because he makes so much sense. It's a joy to read what he has to say about the human condition. It almost makes me want to say, why bother with all the other books; but I can't. I have to expose myself to other perspectives, because it keeps my writing fresh and in focus with the stream of life as it unfolds today. And yet, and yet…"

"I see your point. You're right, of course; because you live in today's world, and you have to stay abreast of the times. But it's nice to have the base you found to stand upon, because it lends gravitas to your writing."

"Penny brought a wire rack home from work yesterday. It's a Hallmark rack which was used for Hallmark cards, but they were going to discard it and Penny brought it home and she put it into her office to display all of my books; and when she put them up, it was quite impressive. And she said to me, "Now when you feel depressed, just go into my office and see what you have accomplished." That was nice of her, wasn't it? She has my sixteen books on display, and it does feel good; but for some reason, my head doesn't bloat up like it used to. I just see my books like something that I just do, like the acorn tree just sheds acorn seeds."

"That's a healthy way to be. But how long did it take you to get here?"

"I know. I know. And this brings me to a point I have to raise with you, the question of what I have come to call the 'vanity gene.' But I will take this up later with you. Right now I have to tend to my morning duties before Penny goes to work; so until later..."

"...I'm back. I did my morning chores (fed our goldfish "Guber" and the ferile cat that has adopted us and who lived under our deck all freezing winter long, snuggled up against the warmth of the house, and the chipmunks and squirrels and sometimes the crows if we have left-over scraps of food), and then took my daily heart medication and saw Penny off to work; but instead of coming back to finish our dialogue, I went out onto the front deck to read one of my Hemingway books that I found in one of my box of books in the basement as I was looking for some more of my Gurdjieff books, particularly Dr. Maurice Nicoll's six volume set called *Psychological Commentaries on the Teaching of Ouspensky and Gurdjieff,* but I couldn't find them and lost my patience looking for them. I took that as a sign that I didn't need them then; maybe later. But I came across *Hemingway, The Toronto Years*, by William Burrel; and I was anxious to start reading it. I wish I had found it while I was working on my own Hemingway Book, *The Lion that Swallowed Hemingway*; but apparently I didn't need that, either. Anyway, I went out onto the deck and read 75 pages before I decided to take a break and complete our dialogue, just to show some grace. So, Padre; I have a few things I'd like to share with you. The first is that while reading about Hemingway's Toronto years, which were his formative years as a writer, I got a flash of insight into my own life; and it is this: I am no longer burdened by my "vanity gene." Believe it or not, I feel like I have been amputated of my "vanity gene," such is the loss so obvious to me now. It's more like "moral surgery," really; and I am no longer shadowed by my own inauthenticity—a very strange feeling, like a whole new feeling of innocence. I don't know how else to express this feeling. But I can tell you this; I also feel angry, because my "vanity gene" deprived me of the spontaneity of my youth. I was so hampered by my "vanity gene" that I never experienced anything "authentically." Everything that I experienced was coloured by the "inauthenticity" of my "vanity gene." What do you think of my new insight into myself? Am I right to believe that my "vanity gene" was hereditary; that I got it from my family?"

The short answer is yes, you did get it from your family. This is the "sin" of your ancestors that has been passed on from generation to generation, and it stopped with you. This was your purpose for being born into your family. You were given the mission to put an end to what you so aptly refer to as your 'vanity gene.' Now that you have put a stop to it in your life, the moral consciousness of your family has been raised enormously; and changes are sure to follow. Yes, I agree with you; you have a new feeling of innocence because you are no longer burdened by your family's karmic burden, which condensed itself into your family's 'chief feature,' to borrow a phrase from your teacher Gurdjieff."

"I have a feeling that my vanity gene is going to find its way into my book on Gurdjieff; but that's for another time. I think I'm going to post my spiritual musing on Joni Mitchell's song 'Both Sides Now' tomorrow morning. I had intended to post my musing 'It's All about Balance', but I'm anxious to see how my Joni Mitchell musing goes over. I'll let you know next week. Okay, Padre; anything you would like to say before I go back to reading my Hemingway book?"

"Live, love, and enjoy your life. Just do what you feel is best for the moment and let the day unfold according to God's will. Have a nice day, my friend."

"Thank you…"

33. I Need a New Receptacle

Sunday, May 10, 2015

"One of the books that I brought up the other day from my boxes of books in the basement (I'm going to have to put my books on shelves one day; it would make rummaging for a forgotten book so much easier!) was Brother Lawrence's book *The Practice of the Presence of God;* and as I was looking through my Amazon Wish List this morning I came upon a book that I have seriously though of ordering because it spoke to me called *The Way of Transformation, Daily Life as Spiritual Practice*, by Karlfried Graf Durckheim, and as I perused the latter book thanks to the Amazon Look Inside feature the idea came to me to talk to you about the concept of a new receptacle for my daily life, *the receptacle being my daily life!* Which is precisely what both Brother Lawrence and Karl Durckheim practiced. So, Padre; after all of my reading and research for my new book, I keep coming back to my own life. I keep coming back to the same old, same old; and it's up to me to make it new, isn't it? This is what I'd like to talk about this morning, if you don't mind. I'd like a fresh perspective, because I've gone through the Seth material in Jane Roberts' books, and a surfeit of Gurdjieff material, and I'm really sick and tired of it all and want to get to solid footing, which brings me back to my own life. Damn damn damn! I can't get away from myself, can I? I have to sit down and write my story—"

"And live your daily life; that's your mission in this world. You were born to discover your own life, not the life of others. You have gone through all the study you needed to find your own life, and you are now entitled to live it. You went to great pains—and I mean, great pains not unlike mine!—to find your true self, and now you are entitled to live and enjoy your life, and write about it. The answer to many questions will be revealed to others as you write the story of your life in your Gurdjieff book, so don't frighten yourself by the books you are reading. They can't do more for you than they have already done; so don't pursue a prey that has already been caught.

Your hunger now is for the creative spirit of your own life, and that you can satisfy in the writing of books and stories."

"And what about the receptacle for my daily life?"

"You know that that receptacle is already. If you put to practice the Tibetan Five Exercises and do a little stationary bike riding and more walking, you couldn't ask for a better receptacle. Try it for one week and see what happens."

"Here's a question for you: who's right? Is everyone right? Is it all a matter of consciousness? What am I to believe?"

"That's the question, isn't it? That's what confuses everyone. Everyone wants that one magic formula that will decipher the mystery of life; but no such formula exists. It's all a question of growth and understanding. Patience is the byword. Make of your life the vehicle of your growth and understanding, and your life will unfold with the grace of a flower. Do not try to rush the growth. It never works."

"Padre, I don't want to go to seed; so I guess I have to take the bull by the horns. But you know what, I'm great at thought but terrible at the execution. I feel I've spent myself finding myself, and I don't have it in me now to live my life the way I would love to live it. I need an infusion of extra energy!"

"I know exactly how you feel. I felt like that many, many times in my life at San Giovanni; and I prayed, and prayed, and prayed. That was my only consolation. And I did my priestly duties. I said Holy Mass and held confessions. And I worked on the hospital concept until it became a reality. I did what I had to do, and so are you doing what you have to do. You write. Look at the books you have out now. They may not be best sellers, but they are out in the ethers because you have put them there; and they do more than you will ever realize, because once a thought is in the ethers—in the River of Life, if you will—it affects the lives of every living person; so don't concern yourself about a large following. Time has its own rewards."

"I didn't get much of a response to my Joni Mitchell musing. What am I to make of that?"

"It is a strange, strange world; and what people do and what people think are not necessarily compatible. People think one thing and do another, and that is what your musings do to people: they force people to think of what they don't want to do, and this has a strange effect upon them. This is your dilemma as a writer."

"I don't want to, but I get it. My writing irritates conscience, doesn't it? People don't want their conscience to be irritated; they want to keep it quiet, asleep to the reality of their purpose in life. That's the sum of it, isn't it?"

"As I said, life is a journey of the self."

"I know. I shouldn't be judgmental. Life is an individual journey, and we all learn and grown in understanding at our own pace. END OF STORY!"

"End of story. Just live by this now and you will do yourself a favor. Do not expect anything from the world, and the world won't disappoint you."

"A good note to end this on. Thank you, Padre."

"You're welcome. And your receptacle—try it for one week!"

"I'll see what I can do—"

"No. That's not good enough. Try it for one week. I don't say this lightly. Try it for one week and see what happens. I implore you."

"Okay…"

34. New Spiritual Horizons

Wednesday, May 13, 2015

"Padre, I'm listening to an interview on *Conscious TV* on You Tube, a spiritual teacher and author called Miranda Macpherson, and the premise of her personal path that she bases of her teaching on came to her in a spiritual experience in a cave in India that was the home of Sri Ramana Maharashi in which a Voice spoke to her, saying: **'Be nothing, do nothing, get nothing, become nothing, seek for nothing, relinquish nothing, be as you are, rest in God,'** which seems to me to speak for the non-dual perspective on life, that place where being and non-being have one transcendent and harmonious point of view; am I correct in this, and if so, is this the new reality that is finally upon us?"

"Yes, and welcome to the new reality. You are a forerunner of this new reality, and in your own writing you reflect the conceptualized consciousness of your own way, which is no less interesting if not much more so than Miranda's because you provide the process of individuating the dual aspects of the self. Yes, you are correct in your understanding."

"Is this why I've been nudged, not strongly enough yet to get me started, but enough to let the idea take root, to write my spiritual musing "The Armchair Guru," which will be the title for my new book of spiritual musings?"

"That will be your theme. It will take a few weeks yet for the seed to sprout to the point where you will act upon it; but it's out now, and you are aware of it, so be on the lookout for new thoughts, new ideas, new concepts to help you give your musing the depth and latitude that it will need for maximum clarity."

"Today is Penny's birthday. She's going to be bringing take-out Chinese for dinner. I got her beautiful yellow roses the other day and she just loves the card. I had to go to three different stores to find the right verse, but it was worth it; she loves the verse. It spoke to her heart, and our relationship."

"You are blessed in your love."

"I have a feeling that you want to come through more. I feel a little restless right now. Can I put this off until later?"

"By all means..."

"I'm back. It is the next morning, *May 14, 2015,* and I did some more research on Miranda Macpherson and one of her teachers A. L. Almaas, who founded the Diamond Approach teaching, and I have something I'd like to run by you: is this Diamond Approach teaching an evolved aspect of Gurdjieff's teaching, which I suspect it to be? It sure seems like Almaas has taken the ball and ran with it."

"You are absolutely correct in your intuition. He has gone to where Gurdjieff could not go because of the premise of his teaching. But even so, you have taken the ball all the way to where it belongs— in the basket of God. You have to tell your story, how you came to your understanding of the individuation process. Trust your own intuition. You have all you need to complete your story. All of your new research will satisfy your curiosity, because you have a mind that needs to be satisfied with new information; but you don't need it to write your story."

"I'm really beginning to see that now. It seems to me that every person who tries to work their spiritual quest into a teaching get to carry the ball, if I may use this metaphor, to shed light on the ONE PATH from their own perspective, from their own experience, from their own understanding of the ONE PATH. The Way is always ONE PATH, which is the way of Soul, and I have yet to read any teaching that gives clarity to the way of Soul as I have experienced. Is this why you keep insisting that I just write my story?"

"Yes. You need not go any further than your own life, your own quest, your own experience with the Divine. Your way is not the only way, but it is the way that offers more clarity than most ways. Just write your story."

"Okay, now I'm going to challenge you, if I may. I know that Spirit is One, and that you are one with Spirit; so, how deep are you going to take me into the consciousness of our relationship? How much are you going to reveal to me? Is our relationship going to take me into the heart of all knowing?"

"Where do you think you are right now? In the heart of all knowing you are yourself; this is what these dialogues are all about."

"Not quite. The door to the deeper regions of Soul have not opened for me yet, and I'd like to know if they are going to open."

"If you're expecting great wisdom to pour into your life like a waterfall, you're going to wait a long time. Wisdom comes as you need it, and not otherwise. This is your path. You must trust your own path."

"This has to do with my 'vanity' gene, doesn't it?

"To a great extent, yes; but not completely. It has to do with the incremental understanding of your process. Your process is definite in its direction, and you have to be definite in articulating it; this is why it comes to you as it does—piecemeal, if you prefer. But still, you have it all in your knowing, because you have been initiated into the mystery of the Self; this is your gift, your grace, your service."

"Alright, I think I'm ready to start meeting those people you said I would be meeting one day; those people that will satisfy my mind's curiosity like some of the books that I read. Don't you think I should be meeting these people now? It would enrich my life immensely."

"Perhaps. It would only expand your circle of understanding insomuch that it would give you a chance to articulate your perspective in personal conversations; but that is not going to happen for a while yet. Perhaps in a year or two it will start to happen with a chance meeting with someone who will give you the intellectual satisfaction that you crave; but it really isn't necessary. When it happens, it happens; and don't waste your time worrying about it. Your life is on its own timetable."

"Okay. I think I'm going to go back to my research until I get enough steam to jump back into my Gurdjieff book. Do you mind?"

"Not at all. Read, read, and then write. That is your way. I look forward to talking with you another day. Ciao, my friend."

107

35. A Quick Word

Saturday, May 16, 2015

"A quick word, if I may Padre. I've been doing some research online on different writers and teachers and "awakened" individuals, and I can't help but feel that after I get over the initial first impressions I'm left with the that same old feeling that where I'm at is where it's at, if I can express it this way without sounding inflated, because for all of their novelty these people are no closer to what I've come to realize and it leaves me wondering why I even bother reading them, or listening to them on You Tube. Do you understand what I'm trying to say?"

"Indeed, I do. You are where you are because the path you have taken is not one that many are familiar with; it is the path of total self-realization consciousness, the path of the individuation of Soul. This is the path that everyone is on, whether they know it or not; but along the way they sidetrack their path to their total self and deem their path to be the valid path for them. It is, and it isn't; and you realize this because your perspective is so far more objective. Just write your story. One day the world will appreciated where you are coming from. You found the secret way, which few people do; and you recognize those that have also found it. That's why you resonate with them so well. Just write your own story and let the chips fall where they may, as you like to say."

"I'm going to get my weekend papers in a short while, and I just wanted to exchange a few words with you. I wanted to inform you that I'm getting quite tired of all this research, but I see the benefits. It is giving me a chance to deflate myself, because I've still got an attitude of vanity that still bothers me; but by listening to all these "awakened" people I get a bit humbled, and this is good for me."

"Yes, it does you a world of good. By the time you are ready to talk with the people, whom you will meet in good time, you will be centered in your own certainty, and this will lend what you say the

authority for others to believe you. Your innocence, despite the lingering traces of that vanity that you keep referring to, will protect you. It is your saving grace."

"I'm off. I'll continue this later, hopefully…"

36. The Damage You Did to Me

Wednesday, May 20, 2015

"I just finished watching the movie of your life story, the English version; almost three and a half hours. I was writing; or, rather, I read the chapters that I had written on my Gurdjieff book and was about to continue with Chapter 7, "The Secret Way of Life," but for some reason I was nudged to look up the movie on your life—an inspiration that was prompted by an email that I got from Amazon.com advertising some books, and at the bottom of the list was a DVD on your life called "Padre Pio Between Heaven and Earth," which prompted me to go online to see if there was a movie on the story of your life on You Tube, and there was; so I sat back and watched it for a hour, until just before noon, and then I went downstairs and put on a minestrone for dinner and came back up and watched the rest of the movie, and the movie ended with your "privileged daughter" standing outside the monastery where you died and she recalls the conversation she had with you. You said to her that day that she brought you your favorite dessert: 'Give to me the gift of your handkerchief so I can wave to you from above,' and she replied: 'Why do you have to wave to me? Where do you have to go?' and you replied: 'Around. To do some damage…' And as the movie ended, with me in tears, I said out loud, 'Well, Padre; you did damage to me. You slew my vanity.' And so, here I am; ready to thank you once again for what you did for me. What a wonderful gift you gave me.!"

"I gave you no more than you deserved. When you came to me full of all the glory of your own accomplishment, I did not expect our book to go where it did; it was only because you took the ball and ran with it, as the expression goes. It could have gone many ways, but because you were genuine in your endeavor it went the way it was supposed to, and your vanity had no chance of survival in the Light of God's Love. You received the gift you came for, even though you had no idea what it was that you sought. You came for a spiritual healing, but the healing came to you in a way that opened you up to the reality

of spiritual conceit; and it brought your novel to graceful closure, and a beautiful ending it was too."

"And now I can continue with my new book. I've been putting it off for one reason or another, which I could not understand; but I think I do now. I had to firm up my conviction in my own belief system, and I did that while watching the story of your life. Good God, how they persecuted you!"

"We need what we need to get to where we are destined to go. I needed to be persecuted just as you needed to die to your old self that kept you from transcending yourself. Despite the fact that you 'created' your own soul, to use Gurdjieff's words—I prefer Christ's concept of spiritual rebirth, though—you were still burdened by a spiritual conceit that would have dogged you for the rest of your life had you not come for a spiritual healing. So here we are now. What do you intend to do with your gift of being the person you have always wanted to be?"

"I guess I'll tell my story. What else can I do?"

"That will be enough for one lifetime. Tell it, my friend. You have a fascinating story to tell. And I promise you, it will be read by millions."

"Let's watch that pumping up. I need ego inflation like a hole in the head. It would be fine just to get the story written, and what happens after that will happen; and that's the best that I can do. So thank you, Padre. You gave me a lot to reconsider today as I watched your life story. You reminded me of the goodness in people, and let the world unfold according to its own design. I'm just a witness, playing my little part in the divine drama of our existence. It's too late to go back to writing, but I'm ready now to continue with Chapter 7. All I have to do is trust my Muse, which I seem to have forgotten how to do. That's why I kept putting off writing Chapter 7, but not anymore. The Secret Way of life is the merciful love of God, and I have to make this clear in a literary fashion within the context of a gnostic understanding of life—which will draw upon all the esoteric wisdom that I can muster. How does that sound, Padre?"

"That's the inspiration you needed to jump back in. Just trust your Muse. It has never failed you yet."

"I will. Until we talk again, *Ciao* my beloved friend..."

37. It's Time to Let Go

Thursday, May 21, 2015

"Padre, I'm going to brush my teeth, shave, and shower and put on fresh clothes; and then I'm going to sit down and have a very serious talk with you about the decision that has been asked of me by the imperative of my own spiritual journey, and I would appreciate your fullest co-operation. Not that I don't get it all the time we talk, but I have to ask because this is very important to me. So, please wait for me until I'm all fresh and ready to talk with you; if you don't mind, that is."

"I look forward to our talk this morning. I've been waiting for this talk for quite some time now. Please, go about your morning duties—"

"Oh! Before I go, let me tell you that I selected a short section from one of our early dialogues to go on the back cover of our new book that Penny is working on for publication, *In the Shade of the Maple Tree.* The piece is taken from Chapter 19, "You Make Me Smile." What do you think of that piece going on the back cover to excite the reader's attention? Was it a good choice?"

"An excellent choice. It speaks to the reader's vulnerability. Now, please go about your morning duties so we can have our talk this morning..."

"Okay, I'm back; and I even put on fresh work clothes because I'd like to go outside today and take care of some of our yard duties. Put out our stone eagle in the water bath, take out our hoses for the front and back yard, and maybe even shovel a wheelbarrow or two of black earth for our lawn. I'll see how the day unfolds. For now, though; let me begin by telling you that I've been researching the controversial material surrounding my spiritual community. I won't mention the name of the spiritual path that I took up after Gurdjieff's teaching, which I don't think is necessary for our discussion because you know which teaching I'm talking about; but because I've always been an eclectic, something about this teaching touched me, which is why I was drawn to it immediately. But now it's time to let go, and that's the purpose of my talk with you this morning. I just don't want to get involved in all the fuss of who said this and who said that; because, when all is said and done, it comes right down to what I trust and believe. And now it seems that I have outgrown my belief in this spiritual path and I have to move on. Is that a good description of what I'm feeling, or is there more to what I've just revealed?"

"Yes, there is more; but you said enough to get you free from the hold that you bound yourself to by your trust in the teaching."

"That's what held me from letting go, wasn't it—my trust? I trusted too much in the eternal truth of the teaching, transferring this trust onto the spiritual leader of the community; but it's time to let go now, because I've always known that the Inner Master was my Higher Self, or Divine Spirit if you will, and I have no reason not to just let go and BE my own path."

"You've been waiting a long time for this. You've always known that one day you would be leaving this spiritual path, and that day has arrived. Do not fear, you have solid ground under your feet. Your books are your truths, and they have stood you in good stead throughout all the talk and rumors in your community; and they will serve you in good stead for the rest of your life."

"I just re-read the final transcript of my last spiritual healing session with you in *Healing with Padre Pio*, as well as the closing chapter, and I had to smile to myself at how we brought that novel home. You certainly revealed much more than I realized, but now it makes much more sense to me. So, thank you Padre."

"You're welcome. Now, back to the issue. You do realize that walking away from a spiritual path is a very serious commitment?"

"I do and I don't. Penny and I have a membership for the rest of the year, but I don't believe we are going to renew it next year. That will be our cut-off date. And for now, we just don't participate any more in our spiritual community. But I cannot help but be grateful for all I learned from this teaching. It served me in good stead, despite the fact that I always felt out of context in my spiritual community."

"Because you were never really in it. You embraced the teaching, but didn't you say that you could never call the spiritual leader of this community your Spiritual Master?"

"That's right. I could never call anyone my Spiritual Master, and I told him that to his face. That's when I had the experience of looking into the Face of God."

"That was Divine Spirit's way of embracing you into the teaching that you had to study to proceed on your destined journey."

"So what do I do now? Do I acknowledge the spiritual leader of this teaching as the high ranking Spiritual Master that he says he is?"

"You know the answer to that question. If the Inner Master is your Higher Self, and your Higher Self is Divine Spirit, what more proof do you need? What he calls himself is his relationship with God, not yours. His mission is his mission, and your mission is your mission; and though he served your mission well, it is now time to walk away and live your own mission in light of your new awareness."

"So it had to be this way, then?"

"Yes, of course. Like Joni's song says, you gained and you lost; it's all life's illusions—Both Sides Now, for the sake of your reader. I too love this song."

"I think I'm almost ready to write my spiritual musing "The Tumbler of Life." I've been polished enough now to step out of the "tumbler" and go my merry way, don't you think?"

"Nice metaphor. Yes, the Tumbler of Life has polished you enough to walk away now—shiny and smooth in your new convictions. By all means, step out of the Tumbler and be yourself. You earned it!"

"I know I have; but there is sadness in my decision."

"And well there should be. You have taken your teaching to heart, as you have all other teachings—especially the parables of Jesus, for which I am very proud of you—and live them; that's what makes you who you are. You walk your talk, and this frightens your spiritual community. You feelings of uneasiness in your community were justly founded, because of the inherent dishonesty of the packaging of the teaching. You embraced the whole package, that's why you have berated yourself the last few years; but it's time to get

114

over that now and move on. You have not lost your respect for the truth of the teaching, but now you are awake to the packaging of the teaching; and you are leaving the package, not the truth of the teaching. The truth of the teaching is yours for life."

"What else is there to say?"

"For now, not much more. You made your point. This is why you have been unsettled this past while; you were smoldering. Well, it's finally out now, and you should be feeling much better very soon."

"Is it possible that my fear of letting go was so deep that it took all of this time and all of the books that I have written to make me strong enough to face my fear and finally let go of this teaching?"

"Yes."

"So there is truth to the built-in fear factor in the teaching?"

"Yes."

"Intentionally so?"

"Yes and no. He was very conscious of what he was doing, but conscious enough of the effect it would have on his spiritual community."

"And now the big question: the initiations. Are they what the community says they are? This is where the fear factor speaks the loudest."

"Initiations are personal. They can only be personal, because you know from your own spiritual journey that there is only self-initiation into the mysteries of life; so, yes the fear factor was built into the initiations to bind the spiritual community and keep followers from defecting. It was a strategic move, and it worked; but now the chickens are coming home to roost, as you have suspected for the last few years. This is why the community has begun to stagnate."

"Here's another big question, if I may. I spelled it out in my penultimate and closing chapter in *Healing with Padre Pio*, but I have to ask you now: Did the affected love that I saw in my spiritual community reflect the shadow side of my spiritual community? Is it the shadow side that I could not stand?"

"It was the shadow side of your spiritual community that could not stand you, because you were too real for them. This was why you always felt out of context. But don't judge them for it,

because they too have their positive side. They just were not as aware of their shadow as you were, or the shadow of their community."

"And is this why I don't have dreams of my spiritual community, and the spiritual leader? Is it because I've transcended my spiritual community?"

"Yes."

"Then why don't I dream of you?"

"Do you have to?"

"I'd love to. Don't you think I've got enough of a handle on my inflatable ego enough yet to have dreams of you and my life of writing on the other planes?"

"You do now; so keep an eye out for your dreams. They will begin to take on a new flavor. I promise you, my good friend."

"Are we friends, Padre?"

"Much closer than you realize. We have been together many times, Orest; in this lifetime, and many others. We work as a team."

"From whence do we come?"

"Your favorite poet said it best: 'From God, who is our home.'"

"Yes, I know that; but you know what I'm getting at."

"I do, but you are not ready for that information yet."

"Still too inflatable, eh?"

"Yes and no. It would serve no purpose now other than to satisfy your curiosity, which could inflate your ego if you let it."

"Padre, I'm getting peckish, as I used to say in my old lifetime in London, England; so I'm going downstairs for a sandwich. But what a life that was. That served me well, even though it proved to be a very hard life."

"Without that lifetime you wouldn't have had to repeat your life now. Because you failed to resolve your issues in that lifetime, you came into your life as Orest Stocco so unresolved that you couldn't continue in your journey; so you resolved to repeat your life to transcend yourself. That's why your second lifetime as Orest Stocco has been so hard. You had to prove yourself, and you did."

"This opens a whole new perspective on reincarnation, doesn't it?"

"Indeed, it does; and your life will be living proof."

"I have to ask you, does the spiritual leader of my community believe himself in his teaching of Godman?"

"That's not for me to say. It is his relationship with God. And you needn't bother your head about it. I never questioned the Pope in my lifetime as a Capuchin priest, and I don't think it would be wise for you to question the qualifications of your spiritual leader. Let the world unfold on its own. You learned what you did from this teaching, and now you are moving on. Let Divine Spirit unfold."

"Fair enough. Leave the tangles and the briars and the foxes and the hens and the wind and the rain and the sun alone; life is life, and that's the enantiodromiac nature of the whole evolutionary process!"

"Well said. Are you happy, now?"

"Relieved. Now, as to our triplex up north. What's happening?"

"It's in God's hands. Trust God, my good friend. Isn't that what you were told in that passage that you are going to put on the back cover of your new book In the Shade of the Maple Tree?"

"Yes, that's the passage; so, trust God, then. But may I ask how?"

"Good question. How can we trust God? Why should we trust God? Because when all is said and done, we have no other choice. Let me explain. The journey to our destined self is, as you rightly concluded, a journey through vanity to humility; and only in our humility are we free to see that God is the giver and taker of all that is, and we have no choice but to trust that God gives and takes for the purpose of God's agenda; and what is God's agenda given your spiritual journey?"

"To grow in the consciousness of God."

"Yes, but does God do anything that will damage God?"

"Are you saying that all is good, no matter what?"

"In effect, yes; but more than that. God serves us, even if we don't serve God; and God always does what's best for us. If you feel that it would be best for your triplex to sell now, God will serve you. Ask God. See what God says."

"You are a humble servant of God. The most humble servant of God that I know, so I'm going to ask you; and I implore you because I know that your relationship with God is reciprocal, if you know what I mean. So, from where I stand today, I honestly think it would do Penny and myself a lot of good to sell our triplex this summer, because it would free us to live the kind of life that we have been dreaming about for a long time—free of the burden of financial anxiety. Can you tell me if this dream is possible or not?"

"Definitely possible, and it's in God's hands. Trust God, my good friend."

"Fair enough. I'm going down for an egg salad sandwich. Until we talk again, Padre. Thank you for our chat today."

"You're welcome."

38. The Greatest Force in the World

Friday, May 22, 2015

"I couldn't sleep and I got up shortly after four this morning and finished watching *The Razor's Edge* that I was watching last night. I was tired last night, drained of my energy, and I decided to go to bed and listen to CBC's *Ideas*. It was featuring Part 2 on Dante, and I wanted to catch it because I was interested in the Italian poet. And this morning rather than read as I usually do in the morning, I decided to watch the rest of *The Razor's Edge*. I wanted to see it again (I've seen it several times over the years), but for nostalgic reasons I had to see it once more because I heard the call to become a seeker in high school when I read Maugham's novel *The Razor's Edge*. At the end of the movie Isabel, who loves Larry but could never have him because he was destined to be a seeker, says to Somerset Maugham who plays himself in the story, "What is he trying to do with his life? What does he hope to find?" And Maugham replies, "My dear, Larry has found what we all want and very few of us ever get. I don't think anyone can fail to be better and nobler and kinder for knowing him. You see, my dear; goodness is after all the greatest force in the world, and he's got it." Thus ends the story of *The Razor's Edge*. And now I'm telling you about it because I had to write something just to get these feelings out. I thought of writing a spiritual musing on the greatest force in the world, but I just wrote a musing a week ago called "Why Be Good?" So here I am, Padre; half a century—*God, has it been that long?*—and my own search done and over with and I'm still moved by Maugham's story despite how superficial it seems to me now after what I had to go through to find myself; but it's still a damn good story, and I'm glad Maugham wrote it because it made a difference to my life, and I'm sure to many others as well. But that's what writing's for, isn't it? After all, the purpose of story is to bear the truth and meaning of life, and when the truth of story touches one's soul the writer has done his job. I guess that's why I write. I want to convey the truth of meaning of life as I've experienced it. I hope you don't mind me prattling on like this, Padre."

"Not at all. And you are correct to believe that The Razor's Edge touched the lives of many people. For its time, it made quite an impression. That's what writers are meant to do, break the trail for the rest of the world."

"I feel that I'm so far ahead of everyone else that the trail I'm breaking in with my writing will be all grown back in again before anyone can discover what I've written. Wouldn't that be ironic?"

"There is humor in what you say, but it won't happen that way; you will be found before the trail gets grown in again. The Internet is an open highway, and once you're online, someone will be sure to find you."

"I suppose, but it does feel lonely sometimes. But I don't want to go down that road today. I want to try to get my life back, however much of it I can get back; but it scares me thinking about it."

"Don't be. Just do what you have to do, and let the day unfold as it will. I am here for you every moment of your day..."

39. A Heavy Heart

Sunday, May 24, 2015

"Padre, I'd like to talk and talk and talk about my heavy heart, but I don't want to talk and talk and talk about my heavy heart because I feel like a fool; but I have to get this off my chest or it will sour me. For over thirty years I believed what I wanted to believe about the spiritual teaching which I cannot even bring myself to name for you (thank goodness I don't have to), but the truth is that it gave me comfort despite how cultish it was taken to be by the world. And where does that leave me today now that I have broken free of the hypnotic spell it had on me?"

"Free to think for yourself. You got what you needed from that teaching, and it did serve you well because you believed in it; this is the mystery and glory and mercy of God, who grants us what we need regardless how it is given."

"So now we get to the question of authenticity. I have always sought to be authentic, and I worked my ass off to get it; but as authentic as I became, there was always a part of me that wasn't real. I sensed this in the marrow of my bones, and I could never figure it out. Is this the source of my inauthenticity? Is it because I believed in a teaching that was not packaged in authenticity?"

"You phrased it correctly. It wasn't packaged in authenticity, but the truths of this on the whole were founded in spirituality; so you gained from it immensely. Do not beat yourself up over this, as the phrase goes. You have broken the spell it had over you, and now you can write with a more realistic perspective. It will come through in all you write, and it will free your ideas to flow more easily."

"I do have a heavy heart, though."

"That won't last long. You have been hurt before, and you suffer your hurts pretty well. This one was a big blow, but you saw it coming. Now that it has come, take it on the chin and make the best of it. Write about it. That's the best way to work it out of your system. Work it into a story, if you can."

Following day...

"I took time off to write a spiritual musing, which came to me unannounced; well, it didn't come unannounced as such, because I beckoned it with my need to clear up my confusion, which I did with my spiritual musing. It's called "The Parable of the Packages," and it relieved me of a lot of pressure. Now we can resume our talk, and I'd like to start with a question: was this teaching responsible for so much disruptive energy in my life?"

"The short answer is yes. It was not founded upon reality, but the reality of the teaching was sound as far as it went; so the energy that you picked up from your spiritual community was always mixed with light and shadow. The disruptive element was the shadow, which you already knew; but now it is confirmed, and you are free of the hold that it had upon you. This is a breakthrough."

"Padre, you know what it means to be called a cuckold in the Italian culture; it's one of the worst things for a man to be called. Well, I can apply this term here with respect to this teaching: it cuckolded me! That's why I feel like a fool."

"Yes, there is that; but what about the benefits. We met, didn't we? Do you think we would have met had you not studied this teaching? What brought you down here in the first place? You moved away from your hometown because of the books you wrote, which were directly the result of studying this teaching; so one thing leads to another, and here we are. Life is a journey of the self from one experience to another, and there are no right and wrong experiences; they are all given to you for your growth and understanding. Can you deny your growth and understanding? It was tainted with the shadow element, but you sifted through that in your writing; so you have nothing to be ashamed about. You took it all in, and you mined the gold from all the dross; and now you are free to move on."

"What bothers me is the depth of my conviction in light of the world's skepticism. The world was right and I was wrong. That's humiliating."

"Didn't you write in Healing with Padre Pio that life is a journey through vanity to humility? Well, this is a perfect example. You are living proof of your own wisdom. You don't get your wisdom

cheaply, my friend. That's the price you have to pay for the wisdom you seek. This is why I said that we are very much alike. I also suffered your humiliation because I could sympathize. I believed implicitly in my Church, and I knew that it contradicted the truth in many ways; but I could not bring myself to question it just as you could not bring yourself to question your teaching, and now you suffer the pain of self-flagellation. Stop it. You don't need to suffer any more. You have realized the benefit of that teaching, and now you can move without that baggage. It served you well, my friend; well enough to free you of the archetypal hold that the shadow of life had over you. Life no longer has this hold on you, because you have seen through life's illusions. Be happy for your freedom."

"Here's another question, then: now that the connection with this disruptive energy has been severed, shouldn't my life and Penny's life flow more freely, more harmoniously, more fruitfully?"

"In principle, yes; and in fact, yes also. This is the gift of having the courage to let go of the shadow side of life. You no longer have to fight that energy. It can't touch you now that you are conscious of its true nature. Yes, your life and Penny's life will be rewarded with abundance. Trust me on this."

"I should tell you now that I think of it, Penny has almost completed the process of getting our first book of dialogues published. It's called *In the Shade of the Maple Tree*. What do you think of this little book?"

"I enjoyed reading it as much as I enjoyed composing it with you. It is an exercise in active imagination with opens the door to real spiritual dialogues with me on this side of life. Don't fret, there's more to what you write than what you want to believe. This is the opposite of your feelings for your old spiritual teaching, because for this teaching you wanted to believe, and you did; that's why you feel like you have been cuckolded by this teaching. I respect your freedom. I would never do anything to diminish it. My job is to enhance it, which is just the opposite of your old spiritual teaching despite what it teaches."

"Did the psychic medium know about this teaching while we were doing my spiritual healing sessions for my book *Healing with Padre Pio*?"

123

"She had her suspicions. You were so convinced though that she did not really know what to believe. You were much too open for her to make up her mind one way or the other. That was your saving grace with her."

"Are we going to work again on another book, one which I would love to call *Padre Pio Talks from Heaven*; is that going to happen?"

"Yes, once you have completed your Gurdjieff book. You have to write that book first so we can get to the new material you will be exploring. I look forward to our new book together. It will prove to be more fascinating than the last. I promise you. I have a copy of it in my hand right now and I wish I could show it to you; but I cannot. You have to begin the process out there first, which will be sooner than you expect. Just keep doing what you are doing. Write and write and write. It will play itself out according to Divine Timing."

"I'd really like to write a story on my awakening from that teaching, which I suspect may be called "The Funeral Service," because this will be a play upon the death of this teaching in my life as the subplot of the real life death of my friend that I wrote about in *The Pearl of Great Price*. Should I write this story?"

"It would be a good way to get it all out of your system. Yes, by all means; when you are so inclined, let Divine Spirit guide you."

"Why my uneasy feelings about my friend's ex-husband and family?"

"No need to feel uneasy. Time will heal them of their wounds. Your tribute went a long way to help them understand your friend. You did her proud."

"I have a sneaking suspicion that my Muse has already begun to imbue me with the theme of my story, giving me an idea on how to start it—by implying in the first chapter my friend's death and the death of my teaching. Both died, and the service was for both; that's how I think I might play it out."

"It would be a great start. It would also demand much more time than it would take to write a short story, because this story would grow on you. It would be a nice little novella for your book Enantiodromia and Other Stories."

"I thought of that. So, I guess I'll just have to wait for my Muse to become impatient with me. Okay, Padre; thanks for the chat. Until we talk again."

"Have a nice day, my friend..."

40. The Simple Way

Thursday, May 28, 2015

"Good morning, Padre. I'd like to chat this morning, to run an idea by you with respect to further dialogues. I've been reading my Jung books again, and I'm moved to dig deeper into the unconscious—my creative unconscious, if you will. I'd like to run an idea by you, if I may—"

"First things first. Good morning, my friend. Yes, by all means; run your idea by me. I look forward to delving deeper into the creative unconscious; if that's the direction you would like us to go."

"I've got two people in mind when I say this, Carl Jung and Neale Donald Walsch; Jung, because of his "confrontation with the unconscious," which he recorded in what came to be *The Red Book*; and Neale Donald Walsch in his talks with God, with a series of books beginning with *Conversations with God*. I'd like to delve as deep as these two men, my inspiration being Jung's "confrontation with the unconscious," because I'd like to probe the depths of my unconscious. I think it's time I did that, don't you?"

"Yes; but like Jung, it would require some degree of commitment. It also would require a letting go that you are too timid to undertake, unless you begin the process with a definite aim in mind. Do you have a definite aim in mind?"

"I think so. As I was reading *Jung, His Life and Work* by Barbara Hannah this morning with my first cup of coffee and later as I read through the opening pages of *The Inner Journey, Views from the Gurdjieff Work*, edited by Jacob Needleman, the idea struck me to concentrate on what can only be called The Simple Way; and by this I mean the essential dynamic of the Way. I don't know if I've expressed this as clearly as I would like, but it has to do with the simple fact that life is the way, and that until we learn how life works we can never live the Way; does this make any sense to you, or am I looking for a diversion to escape my literary obligation to my book *Gurdjieff Was Wrong, But His Teaching Works*?"

"No, it's not a diversion. You've been toying with this idea for a long time now, and it has finally surfaced; so, yes, I'd love to explore it with you. And yes, I do understand what you are getting at. You are tired of all the confusion that the world has made of the Way. It has so many side roads that the Way seems to be lost in all the traffic, and you want to bring it back to the simple path of growth and understanding, if I may express it this way. And I agree with you; the world has become confused with all these side roads to one's true self, with so many getting stuck in the non-self and believe that's their final destination. The goal is for the self to realize its transcendent nature, which is its Divine Self that is both being and non-being and neither; the Soul Self. Yes, we should talk about the simple way."

"Am I ready to talk about it? I keep getting pulled into these explorations of the non-dual consciousness enlightened path that so many people seem to have awakened to but which I mistrust for reasons of my own, because I know that the Soul Self is the flower of our growth and understanding; so how can I go about this exploration with you? Do we begin with a definition of the Way? If I may interrupt myself, Padre; I'd like to ask you another question: is there a buzz going on about my writing? I get the feeling that people are exploring my spiritual musings blog to find out more about my writing. Are my feelings onto something?"

"The buzz started from the day you read your tribute to your friend at her funeral service, and it is now gaining momentum; and it will not stop, because now your book is out, and people will want to explore what you have to say. The tide is coming in, and it will bring your ship home my good friend."

"Why this uneasy feeling, then?"

"You've always been uneasy about becoming successful. Don't let it get to you, because your success is well deserved; and it will be smooth sailing, I promise you. You have come a long way, and your journey will get exciting with new adventures in soul and body. Enjoy your initiation into the final stage of your journey through life. It will be immensely rewarding."

"I don't want to leave this world without another book with you. I want it to be my magnum opus, if that's at all possible."

"You have been granted the time to do it, and it shall be done; but it will not be your magnum opus. It will be just another book that

you can add to your tree of life. Your magnum opus is not written yet. You are working on it now."

"My Gurdjieff book?"

"Yes. This is the book of your life. Your life is your magnum opus."

"I have to tend to my morning duties. So, if you will excuse me we can continue later…"

"I'm back. I sat on the deck after seeing Penny off to work and read a few pages of Somerset Maugham's book *The Summing Up.* I've read it before and loved it very much, because Maugham's writing always encouraged me; and his novel *The Razor's Edge* fueled the call to my true self, so I owe Maugham a debt of gratitude that I can only pay by giving homage to his writing, despite his clever gift of crafting a story so well that he mesmerizes the reader with word pictures to create the effect he wants. Whether that's an aesthetic flaw or not depends up the reader; for myself, I tend to think this is why he was never considered a great writer. He was always lauded as a master craftsman, which I believe he was. But I like reading his *Summing Up,* because he's wonderfully candid about his life and impressions of other people and the world. I think he was a gossip, and I think his stories are a form of gossip in narrative form; a kind of insider's view on the private life of others. That's what gossip is, a look into someone's private life. That's Maugham. He was a master at giving us a look into the private lives of others, a look into their personality that reveals much more than his characters would like to admit. This makes his writing more exterior than interior; and by this I mean that his stories are not organic. They don't grow out of their own DNA, as it were; they grow according to the writer's observations on life and people. A kind of manufactured narrative, not one that springs up of its own accord. And Maugham freely admits that he had little imagination but acute powers of observation. But why am I telling you this?"

"Maybe to get the pot boiling."

"Yes, probably. That's a good way of expressing it. But why do I want the pot to boil, anyway? Perhaps to begin the process of engaging in a dialogue that will take me deeper into myself?"

"That's precisely why you want to get the pot boiling. And this is a good way to go about it. Just let your unconscious write, and write, and write…"

"Okay, that's a good place to end our talk today. I don't have the impulse to write, the desire has waned; so I'm going to sit on the deck and read some more Maugham. Maybe reading about his life as a writer might stoke my writing fire. I can only hope; but I know I'm only avoiding my personal responsibilities. What's a man to do, Padre? Pray, hope, and don't worry?"

"Droll, but sweet. No, just let Spirit move you. That's what it comes down to in the end. And when it feels like Spirit is trying to move an immovable object, you will feel the pressure of duty versus personal pleasure. One must learn to balance both or one will suffer the anxiety of feeling self-deceived. This is a big thing with the world today: too much pleasure and not enough duty. But life is a journey of the self, and each soul will learn its lessons accordingly. This is the simple way, which can be very, very hard in its own way."

"I'm glad you brought our talk back home where it started. Okay, Padre; thank you. Until we talk again."

"Ciao. And may your day be full of grace."

"Thank you, Padre…"

Later in the day…

"I'm back. It's just after 2 in the afternoon, and I'd like to chat some more about my heavy heart which is not so heavy today since I put away all the pictures of the so-called spiritual masters; they're now resting in the closet, and this morning I even took down the big picture of the temple that is the home of this New Age teaching that I lived for more than thirty years, and I have some questions I want to ask you. The first question, which prompted me to chat with you again today, just came to me a few minutes ago: what effect did this teaching have on my unconscious? I ask this question because I feel like I have just come out of a tunnel, and that I am no longer inhibited by the unconscious hold this teaching had on me. Did this teaching inhibit me spiritually?"

"The short answer is yes, but it is very complicated because you were always guided by your Higher Self. Remember, you did not

submit to this teaching's Inner Master because you told him that you could not call him your Master, and he was obligated by Divine Imperative to show you the Face of God because it was God that you sought for your guidance and protection. This is why you saw the Face of God, which shocked the Inner Master of your teaching. But the teaching did you service to concentrate your vanity to the point of unbearable turgidity; that's why you were called for a spiritual healing. You are correct in believing that you were a symbolic forerunner for your spiritual community, and your breaking away will give many the licence and courage to walk away also. You did your community a service that they will be grateful for when they realise it. At first it will shock them, but as they read what you have written, especially your spiritual musing 'The Parable of the Packages,' they will appreciate what you have done for them because it takes an enormous amount of courage and spiritual strength to break the unconscious hold that this teaching has over its followers. But you have no rancor, and that's what makes you a shining light for others to follow. You do us proud."

"And now that I have severed the ties, what can I expect? Will I be free from that uneasy feeling and anxiety that this teaching always gave me?"

"Definitely. And this will free you to be more creative. Your health will even improve and your life will be as abundant as you have always wished. Strange as it may seem, the teaching that was supposed to liberate you only enslaved you; but not you so much as others, because you have always been an independent seeker who could never be contained by one teaching. This was your saving grace, and the bane of your spiritual community. They could not stand your sense of freedom."

"Is this why our friend in Southern Ontario could not finish reading my novel *Healing with Padre Pio*, because she was threatened by the values that I presented in my quest for a spiritual healing?"

"You shook the very foundations of her belief system, and she has not gotten over it yet. She has a long way to go before she sees you for who you are. She is much too vain to see beyond her own values, which she believes to be of the highest spiritual order; but she

also is learning her lesson that life is a journey through vanity to humility. Don't provoke the situation. Let her find her own way."

"I have no intention of provoking her, but her husband calls me regularly to talk; and can he talk. He stays on the phone forever."

"Your energy gives him encouragement. He is much more aware of your integrity than his wife is. She finds you suspect, but he defends you to the hilt. Trust your relationship with him to help his wife find her freedom."

"I'm going to take down the pictures of the other so-called spiritual masters. As I walked by the pictures a short while ago, I looked into their eyes individually and said: 'in over thirty years none of you had the grace to visit me in my dreams, and now you can go into the closet where you belong.' So tomorrow or the next day I'm going to take them down. Which leads me to ask: did they not visit me in my dreams because they were not founded in reality; that they were fabricated by the mythmaking founder of this spiritual teaching?"

"A very good question. No, they were not all fabricated as such; he just gave them different names. But because they were packaged by the fraudulent mythology, they had no power to enter your dreams. You were protected by God, to put it as simply as possible. Your Higher Self was always there to protect you. That's why they never entered your consciousness in your dreams. And this is why the founder of this teaching could not penetrate your field when you met him in a dream; he was baffled by your energy, and try as he may he could not seduce you with his teaching the way he seduced others because you were much too eclectic for him."

"There's a stillness in the air. Is this a foreshadowing of what's to come?"

"Indeed. Enjoy the stillness. There is much more to come."

"Then that's what I'm going to do. I'm going to my front deck to continue reading. I'm reading a Jung book and Maugham's *Summing Up*. Thank you again, Padre; I enjoy your support in my time of need."

"It's my pleasure. Enjoy your reading."

"Thank you."

41. An Important Dream of Lamb Roast and My Hairdresser

Saturday, May 30, 2015

"Good morning, Padre. I'm early today. It's 5:30 A. M., but I woke up from a dream that I'd like to share with you. I hope you can help me interpret it. I didn't place that much importance to it right away, but as I was waiting for the coffee to drip a fresh cup this morning I started reading again (I think this may be the third or fourth time) Jung's book *Man and his Symbols*, and as I read the introduction my dream came to mind and I caught a glimpse of its importance. Here's my dream: I'm at a butcher counter. The lady working behind the counter is the woman who cuts my hair. Her name is Michael Ann. She's a beautiful looking woman and I have always enjoyed her beauty, as I enjoy any woman's beauty. It pleases me to see a beautiful woman, not in a sexual sense; in an aesthetic sense, because a woman's beauty adds to the beauty of life. For me, anyway. And what I noticed about her is that she's flattered to see me. I had made arrangements to pick up a lamb roast, which she has ready for me. I notice that she's wearing more jewelry and make-up than I would have expected, and it flatters me that she wants to look her best for me. She knows that I like her and appreciate her beauty, and I must inspire her to look her best for me. It's like she's reminded by me that she's a beautiful woman. I will provide more context in a moment. Let me finish my dream first. She tells me that she has the roast ready for stuffing. I ask her what kind of stuffing I should use, and she makes suggestions. She shows me the roast and it is fresh and ready to go, wrapped in that fish-netting that meat is often wrapped in. She asked me if I would like it wrapped in tin foil, thinking that perhaps I may be bringing it to someone else; but I tell her that it's for our own use and it would be okay wrapped in ordinary paper. She's very pleasant, smiling, and pleased to serve me. For some reason, I have the feeling that she's very happy to be reminded by me that she's beautiful and special. That's the dream. Now the context. When

Penny and I moved to Georgian Bay I had trouble finding someone to cut my hair. I've always had trouble getting a haircut that pleases me; but from the very first haircut, Michael Ann, the woman in my dream, who worked at a Beauty Salon in Elmvale, gave me the very best haircut of my entire life; and she remained consistent until two years ago when she quit her job to be a stay-at-home mom; and I never got another good haircut again. Until last fall when I stopped by her house and asked if she did home haircuts. She did, and I got my last haircut before winter set in. Now it's spring and my hair is long and I needed a haircut badly. I always let my hair grow long. I have this notion that I'm like Samson. When my hair is long I've got my strength. Well, not really; I just say that to justify not getting my hair cut so often. Anyway, Penny and I were driving into Midland yesterday to look for spring bedding flowers and I stopped in at Michael Ann's and made an appointment for Sunday at 11 o'clock. That's tomorrow, and I can't wait to get my hair cut. Since she cut my hair so often we know a little bit about each other. She divorced her husband and married another man. They have children from their separate marriages. Her husband is a truck driver and sometimes hauls long distances. They bought an old two storey house and seem quite happy. And when we stopped in yesterday she smiled and was happy to see me. I'm surprised how quick she was to set the appointment for Sunday morning. It was Friday when we dropped in and I asked if she could cut it that day or Saturday, but she instantly replied Sunday at 11 A. M. I dropped in last weekend to see if she was free, but they had gone camping for the weekend to Six Mile Lake. Anyway, I'm going for my haircut tomorrow. Now here's what I think about the dream. At first I didn't pay that much attention to it, but as I read the introduction to *Man and his Symbols* I was reminded of how important dreams are, and that dreams are not all about symbols as such; as Jung tells us, dreams are the language of the soul. Soul speaks to us through our dreams, and my unconscious was telling me something important with this dream; and instantly the lamb roast took on a very significant meaning. The whole dream suddenly spoke to me. I don't quite have the full meaning yet, but I think I caught a glimpse of what my unconscious was telling me. Lamb is very important as a symbol. Here are some sayings that attest to this: "pure as a lamb," "innocent as a lamb," and "sacrificial lamb." I remember you telling me that I would offer myself up as the "sacrificial lamb" when I wrote my last chapter to *Healing with Padre Pio*. My chapter was called "The Vanity of All Spiritual Paths," and I didn't know how to write the truth about my spiritual community; and you told me to offer myself up as the sacrificial lamb, which I did, and the chapter came out brilliantly. It brought the novel to wonderful and satisfying closure. In fact, you even comment that you were "content and satisfied" with what we had accomplished. So, Padre; here's what I think about my dream now. I told you the other day that Penny and I have walked away from our spiritual community because after writing my book *The Pearl of Great Price* I saw that I no longer needed my spiritual community and felt ready to walk away from it. I need not go into too much detail here. I will do so in a story I hope to write ("The Funeral Service" is my working title), but after doing online research for several days on the founder of this New Age teaching that I've been living for over thirty years I learned that he was a fraud, and he has been exposed as a liar and plagiarist which a PhD student wrote about in a paper he was writing which evolved into a book called *The Making of a Spiritual Movement,* and for some reason I feel that my dream is connected with Penny and I walking away from this spiritual teaching. Penny has always been uneasy about our spiritual community, but that's a long story; anyway, we walked away several days ago and I took down all the pictures of the Spiritual Masters and the Spiritual Temple in Minnesota, which is the spiritual home of this New Age Religion of the Light and Sound of God, and I feel sanctified for dropping this teaching now. And I think the lamb roast is my inner self, the creative unconscious, telling me that it approves of what I have done. I have sacrificed my spiritual teaching and my dream is telling me that I have gotten all the good, purity and innocence out of it that I can get, and it's time to move on; and Michael Ann, who cuts my hair, is souls' way of telling me that life— the beauty of life—is serving me my lamb roast. In other words, I think Soul is telling me that everything is okay. I was true to the spiritual teaching all of these years, despite the fact that it is hollow in its fraudulent mythology (which I did not know about and only learned about with my research recently), but the truths of the teaching were well-founded, and the roast lamb tells me that they will serve me well in my new life without the teaching. The lamb roast is the sacrifice of the spiritual teaching that I lived for more than thirty years. What do you think?"

"First, good morning. Yes, it was a wonderful dream. Soul did speak to you in the way you have interpreted the dream. It is your ticket to the freedom you sought but could never get while living this teaching. The teaching has been sacrificed to your freedom. You are correct in saying that the lady butcher/hairdresser is life in its beauty which you have always appreciated and the lamb is the sacrifice of the teaching and all together Soul is confirming your decision to go it alone. This is, after all, the title of this book, is it not—The Man of God Walks Alone?"

"It is. But here's the curious thing. Last night I finished reading the Jung memoir by Barbara Hannah on the front deck, and what a pleasant read it was too because it was such a beautiful spring evening, and the thought struck me to read *Man and his Symbols* next; that's why I picked it up this morning. It's like I'm meant to get back into paying attention to my dreams again. It's like now that I have walked away from the guidance of the Inner Master of the New Age Religion of the Light and Sound of God, I've got to pay more attention to what Soul has to tell me by way of dreams. It's like I am free now to listen to my own guide!"

"Exactly. This is why your dream felt like you were in the butcher shop of your old hometown of Nipigon, in the original grocery store where your mother shopped all those many years ago; back to your roots, as it were."

"I was going to mention that feeling of being in that old grocery store in my old hometown of Nipigon. So, I'm back to my roots now—and long before I even heard of this New Age teaching. In fact, have I gone so far back as my first parallel life in my hometown? Did I go back that far, because you did tell me that I have lived my same life before in my hometown?"

"Yes, all the way back to your first same lifetime. This dream is much more meaningful than you realize. The lamb roast is your ticket to spiritual freedom from that old lifetime. The lamb of life has been sacrificed for your freedom in that roast that you received in your dream. It's a blessing, my good friend; a wonderful blessing indeed. You do me proud."

"Thank you. Now I'm ready to post my spiritual musing "The Parable of the Packages," in which I declare to the world why I walked away from this New Age Religion of the Light and Sound of God which I lived for over thirty years. I am going to post as soon as we have our little chat."

"Good. Let it be known to the world why you walked away. Your musing is very well balanced, and it tells the story in a way that can be appreciated by everyone, even those who belong to this teaching."

"Well, the facts are out there; it's all a matter of personal decision whether one wants to stay in the teaching or not knowing what we know about it now. But I keep asking myself, why did the founder of that teaching lie? Why did he create a fraudulent mythology to launch his teaching?"

"That's a long and complicated story, and between him and his God. He was a driven man who had to prove himself, and he chose the world stage to make his mark. He wanted to prove to the world that he was more than what the world made of him. It's all a question of vanity versus humility. That's the gist of his story."

"I don't know what to say, Padre. I honestly don't."

"Don't worry about it. Get your haircut tomorrow and enjoy the beauty of life free from the hold that this spiritual teaching had on you. You can walk away proud of your accomplishment. You were loyal to the teaching, and you have absolutely nothing to be ashamed about. On the contrary, you should be proud."

"I got the impression that I have been offered "the lamb of life" with my dream; that life has sacrificed itself to me as I had to sacrifice my own life to find my life, as Jesus said one should to gain the pearl of great price. Is that an honest interpretation of my feelings?"

"You have put a smile on my face. Yes, you sacrificed your life to gain your life, and now the lamb of life has offered itself to you. This is the heart of your dream message. Soul is saying to you, 'I offer myself to you. Eat me. I am yours.' Which is the same as life saying, 'I am offering myself to you.' And life in this context means the innocence, the purity, and goodness of life."

"Wow! That's a powerful dream, then!"

"Indeed, my friend. Now post your spiritual musing and enjoy the beauty of the day. You have earned it. Until we talk again..."

"I'm back. As I was reading *Man and his Symbols* after I posted my musing I thought of the lamb roast in my dream; and it occurred to me that the lamb roast had been cut in such a way so that it had a deep cavity for filling. That's why I asked the lady butcher/hairdresser what I could put in for stuffing; and she made suggestions but I could put whatever stuffing I desired. Well, it occurred to me that the offer of the lamb roast in my dream is a message that I can put into the cavity of the lamb whatever I choose, like life is telling me to have my pick; am I correct in this interpretation, or does it mean something more?"

"You're correct. Life has offered itself to you in the symbol of the lamb roast, and you can have your choice of stuffing; whatever you desire. It's life telling you that you are free to enjoy your desires without having to sacrifice them anymore. This is the central message of the dream. You have no need to feel guilty for life's sweet pleasures. The innocence, and goodness, and purity of life is yours to enjoy; and your unconscious has given you sanction to enjoy the rest of your life."

"Such a simple dream, so much meaning!"

"The language of Soul is very deep."

"So it seems that I have been called to a new imperative, to read and study my dreams; and I can tell you why, even. The idea came to me to prepare to round off and complete my novel *The Waking Dream*, which has Carl Gustav Jung as a central character. Is this what this is all leading to, to complete this novel?"

"Yes, to prepare you so you can do that novel justice. It is one of your best books, but it is not complete. You have to fill in your relationship with Jung in this story; this is why you have been called back to your dreams."

"But I've got to get my Gurdjieff book written first."

"You will. One book at a time, my young friend."

"Okay, Padre. Now I can get on with my day."

"Ciao for now, then..."

Following morning...

"Good morning, Padre. I didn't want to open up a new chapter with this dialogue, because it's just a follow-up on yesterday's dream about the lamb roast and my hairdresser. I got another lamb reference yesterday while I was driving into Midland to pick up my Saturday papers that I often said to Michael Ann, "shear me down," because my hair was so long and curly like sheep's wool. And the moment I thought of this it came to me why my unconscious used Michael Ann as the symbol to speak to me. As the butcher/hairdresser, she symbolized both sides of life. Life sheared me and life provided me with a lamb roast. Life took and life gave. Both sides now, just like Joni Mitchell's song that I wrote about in one of my musings. This dream has more depth than I realize."

"The language of Soul speaks for the All, and it encompasses every aspect of the dreamer's life. You dream does symbolize both sides of your life, but did you notice that it spoke to you encouragingly? Soul always speaks to encourage the dreamer, telling him or her what they need to know. You needed confirmation on your decision to leave your spiritual path, and your unconscious provided you with the images to clear away any doubt that you did the right thing."

"I still can't get over why that man would fabricate such an elaborate myth just to have the privilege of creating his own teaching. That's beyond my grasp. Can you enlighten me, please?"

"His motive was not malicious. It began with good intentions and got away on him. He wanted to bring out a spiritual teaching that was different than any other but true to the truth that he had discovered. He needed a 'package,' as you correctly surmised; but his 'package' kept getting more and more elaborate, and then it got away on him and he couldn't stop. That's the story of this man's life. He could never harness his enthusiasm. He was brilliant in truth seeking, but his brilliance got in the way of truth telling; and the two are worlds apart."

"What's keeping me from getting into my Gurdjieff book?"

"It's like going to confession. You never did like going to confession because you had to face what you did not like about yourself. The same with your Gurdjieff book, only here you don't want to re-live your quest for your lost soul. Once was enough for you. But

you have to go back there to tell your story. And be as thorough as you can because, as they say, 'God is in the details.' Or, to be consistent, it would be better to say here that 'the devil is in the details.' Actually, both; and this is the tapestry of your story, because you found the devil out and in the process found your lost soul. It is a rich story worthy of telling, and YOU MUST SEE IT THROUGH."

"Yes, I know; but I'm running out of steam."

"Didn't you just read that your hero Carl Jung wrote some of his best books when he was in his seventies and eighties? Didn't he write one of your favorite books, Memories, Dreams, Reflections in his eighty-fourth year? You still have a long way to go yet, my friend; so don't put it off. JUST DO IT."

"DOING is the operative word. Okay, Padre; thank you for the pep talk. I'm going to slide into my day. I'm going to shower and wash my hair when Penny goes for her walk, and later I have to go for my haircut at 11 o'clock. I'm going to see Michael Ann, and I'm going to have her 'shear' me down. Until we talk again, but only if I have something to say. *Ciao* for now..."

42. My Muse Strikes Again

Sunday, May 31, 2015

"I didn't think I'd be back this morning, but I tried and couldn't get into my Gurdjieff book. I got lost trying to find something Jung said. I thought it was in *The Red Book*, but I couldn't find it; and I gave up. I figured it wasn't meant to be at this time, and I tried to move on; but I just couldn't get into the flow of my story. My chapter is called "The Secret Way of Life," but it seems to be waiting for something to happen before I get into it fully. I don't know what. In any event, while Penny was having her morning coffee with me she was reading *Anderson's Fairy Tales*, which she finds very interesting; and she was reading about the Parable of the Talents in the fairy tale called "Psyche,", and no sooner did she tell me about the fairy tale of the artist who buried his "talent" and I was struck by my Muse to write my third book on Christ's parables, the first being *Why Bother? The Riddle of the Good Samaritan,* and the second being *The Pearl of Great Price.* This one will be *The Parable of the Talents.* I've been waiting for my Muse to strike me with the idea for my next book on the parables of Christ, and it happened this morning because of the certainty of my feeling. With this parable I can bring to bear the simplicity of Christ's teaching, which few people can because it presupposes a gnostic understanding of the secret way. This I can do, and I'd like your professional opinion; and by professional, I mean from your own gnostic understanding of the secret way, which you realized through suffering. Would, you please?"

"Yes, by all means. The difficulty about the secret way is that it is so simple, as you have come to realize; but making the secret way clear is not so simple. That's the paradox of the secret teaching. I enjoyed our work on our book Healing with Padre Pio (yes, I did say our book), because you fathomed the secret way, which few people do; that's why we had such resonance. But to answer your question, I do believe you were stricken by your Muse to write your next book of Christ's parables on the Parable of the Talents because this parable best describes the art of what in Healing with Padre Pio you called

'the selfless self.' This concept is next to impossible to communicate, but you did an excellent job in the novel; and now you have been called upon to do this concept justice in The Parable of the Talents. This is one of my favorite parables, and I cannot wait to be with you when you write it. I will be prodding you on, as I often do. It will happen while you are working on your Gurdjieff book, and your spiritual musings. You need that to keep you engaged in your creative process, otherwise you shrivel up and whine and whine; and you know how much whining I can take before I step back and let you work it out."

"Alright, let's not get carried away. Considering everything, my whining isn't all that bad. I do get carried away sometime, but that's only because I'm such a procrastinator. I've been stricken with what I can simply call the 'Tomorrow Virus,' which simply means that I keep putting things off until tomorrow, but as you well know this is a fantasy because tomorrow is just an excuse to not do it today. Tomorrow never comes, as you say, because there is only today. So the 'Tomorrow Virus' can make me pretty sick of myself, and rather than admit it to myself as I should I whine and whine. And that's my story. Maybe that's why my Muse struck me with the idea for my next book on Christ's parables?"

"Yes, I would agree; because as you get into this book you will recall memories of when you were a DOER. This will inspire you to DO again, which is the only cure for the 'Tomorrow Virus.'"

"I did catch a glimpse of my first chapter, which would be about a simple explanation of the secret way. This would be my template, and from there the parable of the talent can unfold with all the grace of soul's awakening. You said that this is your favorite parable. Can you tell me why? You do realize, of course, that by asking you this question I am hoping to delve deeper into the creative unconscious?"

"Of course, and you have a right to start delving deeper. It's only fair to tell you, however, that the deeper you delve the more you will learn about yourself."

"And about you, too!"

"Touché. Yes, of course. Well, the parable of the talents is my favorite parable because that's what Jesus' life was all about. He gave the ultimate in his death on the cross, which I tried to emulate

with my own life. My greatest accomplishment was my efforts to get the hospital built and up and running. That was my greatest legacy, of which I am very proud."

"For the record, your hospital is called, in Italian, *'Casa Sollievo della Sofferenza,'* which means 'House for the Relief of the Suffering.' And what a legacy you left behind, not to mention all the souls that you touched with your love and compassion. You were a living model for the parable of the talents, and I can't wait to have you stand behind me while I write this book. I'm looking forward to it now, which means that I can expect my Muse to start giving me chapter titles."

"I particularly like the idea for your first chapter. If I may make a suggestion, call it The Simple way of Christ Revealed"

"Christ or Jesus?"

"I prefer Christ, because Christ speaks to the secret way of life. After all, Christ is Divine Spirit made manifest in Jesus, so by revealing the simple way of Christ you reveal the mystery of the secret way."

"But didn't Jesus say, 'I am the Way, the truth, and the life'?"

"True, but that would only confuse your reader. Clarity is what you want, and you want to make clear that the secret way is Divine Spirit. Jesus was a man who made manifest the way of Divine Spirit; that's how he became the Christ"

"And the theme of my book *The Parable of the Talents* would be about the individuation of Divine Spirit? But not quite so esoteric. I would explain that by living the secret way one individuates the consciousness of Divine Spirit and grows in their divine nature. Is that the gist of it?"

"Yes. And you will be giving many examples of this with your own life and the life of others, from your reading and personal experiences. The object of this book, which will be what you humorously referred to as your post-spiritual community book, will be to explain in the simplest terms possible the very complex dynamic of soul's individuation through being and non-being. This will be the purpose of The Parable of the Talents. I look forward to how Divine Spirit (your Muse) works it out for you. I know the result, but the result is not mine to share with you. It will be what it will be according to your own will and creative expression."

"Let's not be coy. Tell me, anyway."

"Better than you can expect with what you are going into the book with. The book will reveal itself to you as you write it."

"Fair enough. I have to go for my shearing now. Maybe when I get back from my haircut we can talk some more. *Ciao* Padre."

"Ciao, my friend."

43. Life Is a Muddle

Tuesday, June 2, 2015

"Life is a muddle, Padre. That's the thought that I woke up with this morning. I was listening to the radio (I can't sleep without the radio; that's why I have to sleep in a separate bedroom so Penny can get some sleep) and some radical woman preacher was talking, and the more she talked the more I saw how she was trying to work her way through the muddle of her life. She was a good person, but very confused; and she was trying to find her way with Christ's teaching. Good for her, but listening to her was exhausting. It's exhausting listening to people trying to find their way out of the muddle of their life; but at least they're trying. I guess I'm telling you this because I just stepped out of the muddle of my life with that spiritual teaching that I was living. I lived this teaching for over thirty years, and now I find out that it has a fraudulent history; and I've got a heavy heart. I'm not as angry as I should be, or have a right to be; but that's only because I got a lot of good out of this teaching. But there was always something wrong, and I could never put my finger on it. Now I know what was wrong. This teaching was a mixture of two energies: the false and the real, and I've always been at odds with the false energy of this teaching. Which is why I never resonated with my spiritual community. Well, I'm out now; but I don't mind telling you that I feel like a damn fool. I embraced this teaching without questioning it. I took the word of the founder of this teaching for granted. That's how convincing he was in his lies. Now what, Padre?"

"Now you get on with your life. It's water under the bridge. You have moved on. Don't let it get to you. If you dwell on it, you will only berate yourself; and you have no need to do that. You learned what you needed to learn, and you can take that to the bank. Write about it. That's how you get everything out of your system. Write your funeral story. Start it. It might get you out of your funk."

"I have to concentrate my energies. I've let myself scatter the past few days, and I can't write with focus. I've let myself go, and I could hate myself for that. I'm afraid to start my funeral service story.

I don't know what's going on with my life. I'm on the edge of something. It is 5:20 A. M., and I could use a cup of coffee; so I'm going downstairs to put on the coffee pot. Please excuse me."

"By all means..."

"I'm back. Penny has joined me for coffee because she has to be at work this morning for 7. A. M. She has to help do the inventory for the card department of the Wal-Mart store in Wasaga Beach. Normally she doesn't go to work until 8:30. She's reading her *Anderson Fairy Tales* book and I'm chatting with you. I hope you don't mind the company."

"I appreciate the company. Penny is the love of your life, and your Muse; and you get along so well with her that it makes me proud. I welcome her into our space, as the phrase goes. I see that she has warmed up to Healing with Padre Pio. It took her a while, but she's getting over what bothered her about the book; but we won't go into that here. Perhaps another time."

"How independent can you be in our talks? By this I mean a distinct identity apart from the archetypal energy of my own creative unconscious?"

"That's a good question. Perhaps there is no distinction. The only way to find out is to jump in and let the bottom fall out, as Jung did with his confrontation with the unconscious. He took the plunge. Maybe you need to take the plunge too."

"Because of my 'automatic' writing experience, I'm leery to take this kind of plunge. That's why I'm so cautious in our talks."

"It's good to be cautious. But on the other hand, the cautious people don't risk anything, and they never get to experience the vibrating pulse of life. They insulate their life with the buffer of caution, and they never fully appreciate what life can offer. The risk in taking the plunge in any dimension of life is that one will experience the full force of life, be it for the good or the bad; and the experience will give one the energy to grow in understanding. Better to risk life than let it pass you by; but that's my perspective from here. It wouldn't have been my perspective when I was alive. I tended to be very conservative when I was a Capuchin priest."

"You beliefs may have been conservative, but your life was anything but conservative. It was extreme in every way. And in the extreme, you experienced the energy of life at its most dynamic. That's how your life could be such a force for miracles. Divine Spirit flowed through you despite yourself. That's why you said, 'I'm a mystery to myself.' You didn't understand how Divine Spirit used you, but you knew it did; and you prayed to be of service to Jesus. This was your life. This was your way. This was your purpose. What a life, Padre!"

"Yes, it was quite a life. Divine Spirit used me, and I could not get enough of God; that's why I endured the pain. It was my glory."

"Not many people understand that, do they?"

"No. You have to be initiated into the mystery of the Way to understand the glory of God. You understand, that's why we're very much alike."

"Tell me, if you will, is it possible to concentrate the energy of God, the inspiration that flows through me? Can I focus this energy?"

"Of course you can. You know this. You've done this many, many times. This is your forte. You initiated yourself this way. Just go back to your roots. That's how you can focus your life and get into serious writing again."

"Go back to my roots? My Gurdjieffian discipline?"

"Yes, and your Royal Dictum discipline (partially, not totally as before), and your Jesus ethos; they served you well."

"Those were good days. I suffered, but they were good days. To use your word, they were my glory days. I grew immensely when I confronted myself and overcame myself. That was my forte, as you say."

"And it still can be. You're much older now, and your body cannot support the kind of effort you would like to make; but you can still focus your energies and concentrate them to that point of laser-like thought. That's what you miss. Give yourself a chance and try to bring your energies back into focus. They will serve you very well. They always have."

"My mind understands, but my heart has been damaged, if I may play upon the metaphor of not having the heart for it. My health has a great deal to do with my funk. I never want to admit it, but my damaged heart has dampened my ardor. In all frankness, I really don't have the heart for what I love to do."

"We can go on about this until the cows come home. Pick a spot and stand still and do nothing or step out and do something. Between doing and not doing is a dangerous place. It's the place where anxiety breeds the fastest, and before you know it you are drowning in anguish. Pick a spot and stand still. Read, write, just do something; don't torture yourself with what you can't do and what you want to do. That's the devil's playground."

"I couldn't agree more. But it's getting started. That's why I'm chatting with you this morning. I'm trying to collect myself by focussing on this dialogue. The more I chat with you, the more I tap into the well; and the more the water of eternal life flows through me, the more complete I feel. *N'est ce pas?*"

"Well said. Yes, the more you tap into the well of your creative energies, the more complete you feel. Then take this energy and pour it into your book. Go there this morning and get into your story. You're only putting off what you know you have to do; so just do it."

"Not quite yet. I have a few more things on my mind to run by you. Let's clear up this picture that I have of my old spiritual community. The energy of my old spiritual community—and I call it old now because it seems so far away—was never really harmonious; it was always uneasy, like I was waiting for something to break through, something I didn't particularly want to see. Was this the shadow of the spiritual community? Was this the underside, the lie of this teaching?"

"You hit the nail on the head. The shadow was always lurking, waiting to break free; that's why the uneasy feeling. You sensed it, and Penny sensed it even more; that's why she hated going to the spiritual functions."

"But thirty-some years to work my way out of this teaching? And only because of the energy that I tapped into with my book *The Pearl of Great Price*? My God, if it took me that long and the power of the energy of my book, what will it take other initiates of this teaching to see through the lie?"

"It's not your place to say. They are on their own journey to spiritual self-realization, and who can say what they are getting out of it. Every lesson one gets is for that individual, not for another. Life really is an individual journey."

"I know this. I'm just being me. I want so desperately to blame somebody, but I know that life is what it is and I can't really do anything about it. You know, Padre; it doesn't get any simpler, does it? It gets more complex. Life is a muddle!"

"That's how we started this talk. Yes, life is a muddle; but as you work your way out of the muddle you know that life is a muddle. There is a difference when you are in the muddle and don't know it. You can see the muddle, that's what makes you different. And that's why it bothers you watching people working their way out of the muddle of life. You feel sorry for them, but you know that it's their struggle; and so you get upset with yourself. Don't. Everyone is where they have to be to learn what they have to learn so they can become what they are meant to be; and that's the bottom line of this story. Capisce?"

"Wow! You're using the word *capisce* on me? You know how strong that word is? Of course you do. I love it, but it can be quite damaging to others. Penny hates that word. And so do most people who know what it means. Yes, Padre; I *capisce*. Compassionate indifference, then? That's the answer, isn't it?"

"Compassion, but not indifference; compassion with loving commitment to adding to the understanding of life by telling the story of how you worked your way out of the muddle of life. That's your legacy to the world. You are one of the lucky ones who found the way out, and that means a lot to those who are looking for the way out of the muddle of their lives. Your writing liberates people from the hold that life has over them. Don't be indifferent to their plight, compassionate or not; offer them the clues and strategies they need to find their own way out. That's what Gurdjieff did for you. He jumped in with his belief system, and he provided a way out for many seekers. That's what the founder of your old spiritual community did too; he founded a teaching that gave people hope. But we won't go there yet, because your wound is still too tender. Suffice to say that his motive was good, but he got lost in the execution of his model teaching; and it got away on him. Now the lie is too big to dismantle, and it will go on until it collapses of its own dead weight."

"That won't be for a long time, because it has a solid foundation in its temples of worship throughout the world. But who knows, really?"

"Things can change in the blink of an eye. The most that man can do is live his life the best he can with what he has and muddle his way through, as the expression goes. That's life. But it's nice to have people point the way out of the muddle, isn't it? Look at what Gurdjieff did for you?"

"Yes. And what YOU did for me! YOU slew my vanity. YOU spared me spiritual angst that I would have suffered for the rest of my life because of the lie of my spiritual community, and I can't thank you enough for working with me on my novel *Healing with Padre Pio*. It was my way out of my spiritual muddle. God, I don't know what would have happened had I not met you through the psychic medium who channelled you! You came to her for many reasons, but I know now that I was one of those reasons; and I'm so grateful for your reconciling energy that I don't know if I can ever make it up to you for what you did for me. Perhaps by publishing our chats, and perhaps another book with the psychic medium. I sure hope that comes to pass. Is it going to come to pass?"

"Yes. After you write several other books. This being one of them. You have come a long way since our book together, and you will be going into our new book together with such an open mind that many vistas will be granted you. It will prove to be an exciting book, way beyond your expectations. I promise you."

"I can't wait. I'm going to scan my mind to see if there's anything else I want to run by you this morning, and then I can get on with my day…One question, please; and then I can get on with my day. Why did I feel that my hairdresser was uneasy with me when she cut my hair?"

"You're flattery put her off. She didn't want to encourage any personal talk because of how her husband feels. You were correct in feeling that her husband is a jealous type, and you did right to keep it short. Just let it be. She has her own life and her own path and she knows how deep a person you are. She's grateful to know you, but she can't afford to be too personal with you. That's why she felt uneasy. Don't worry about it. No damage was done."

"You're telling me what I already know, aren't you?"
"In effect, yes; but you needed confirmation."
"And how true is it?"
"Time will prove it true. I promise you."

"Okay. Until we talk again, thank you."

"You're welcome…"

44. Proof Copy of Our Dialogues

Friday, June 5, 2015

"Good morning, Padre. We got the proof copies of *In the Shade of the Maple Tree*, the first volume of our dialogues; and I have to tell you, I'm very grateful that we did this, because they tell me how much I love talking with you. It's not so much that I whine and moan a lot, it's in your response to my situation that delights me; you seem to be so fresh in your answers, and always positive. You never, ever give me a negative perspective. You always see the positive side of everything, and this puzzles me. Tell me, how do you do it? Are you so centered in love that there is nothing else for you? Is the negative just another side of love and you don't show the dark side but the love side, if that makes any sense? After all, all is one; is it not? And if all is one, then the negative has to be love also?"

"Indeed it is. First things first, though. Good morning, my friend. Yes, I also enjoyed our first book of dialogues. I enjoy the interaction. It shows all of you, in your strengths and weaknesses; and people like to see both sides of people. This is a much better book than you thought it would be, and it will be a very enjoyable read as well as very informative. You do have a way of bringing out the freshest point of view on things, and people like freshness. That's the trouble with the world, too much of the same old same old; and now, what do you have in mind?"

"Well, if you really want to know I've still got a heavy heart over leaving my spiritual path after I found out that it was founded upon a fraudulent premise. I can't for the life of me understand how a man could fabricate a spiritual teaching—well, not fabricate the teaching, but compile it as he did and then found it upon a foundation that is a pack of lies. That really bothers me."

"Yes, that does bother you; but what bothers you more is not figuring this out for yourself a long time ago. You trusted too much. This has always been your problem that has gotten you into trouble over and over again; but it's better to trust than not to trust. The

lessons learned from the former are far superior to the lessons learned from the latter. Not trusting makes one hard and insensitive. Trusting opens the heart to love and understanding. You understand why that man did what he did to make a living. He created a teaching to get by, and in the process gained a large following and made more money than he dreamed of; and now the teaching has become a New Age religion and it is here to stay for a long while. But you learned what you had to learn and it was time for you to walk away."

"Is that why I was pulled into my spiritual healing sessions with you, so my relationship with you could give me the strength I needed to break away from my spiritual community?"

"That was definitely one reason. There were others. We had worked this out before you went back into your same life over again to achieve a different outcome, and yes; you are right to think what you just did, the different outcome was the reason we had to meet in the spiritual sessions you had with the psychic medium. I wanted to help you see that you had outgrown your spiritual community so you could walk away on your own terms. Mind you, your spiritual community did not make it any easier for you to stay; but be that as it may, the end result is that you finally saw through the game and are free to walk your own path."

"I feel I have a lot more to say about this teaching, but not yet. I may get to the heart of the matter in the story I plan to write, 'The Funeral Service,' which may be a novella for my book of short stories *Enantiodromia*; but I'll have to wait and see. I just don't know where I'm going with that yet. But I do want to thank you for our dialogues, because if this second volume reads anything like the first I'll be more than delighted. I just like the exchange that we're having. It feels fresh and not like a reflection of my own mind. Is that what you meant by asking me to wait and see how it would turn out, whether you were real or a projection of my own unconscious; an archetypal St. Padre Pio, if you will?"

"Yes. As always, you have to decide what is real and what is not, just as you decided about your spiritual teaching. You accepted it as real until you learned that it's not real and founded upon a false foundation. The truths of this teaching are drawn from ancient sources that are founded in personal experiences that certain spiritual seekers had, but how the founder of your spiritual teaching put them

together was false and misleading; and you found this out on your own. Now you don't believe in the foundational basis of this teaching, and you walked away. But you had to have this teaching to see you through that part of your journey. You don't need it anymore, so it served its purpose. That's why you have ambivalent feelings about this teaching. It served you well, but now it's time to move on."

"I know, but I still cringe at what a fool I made of myself because of this teaching. I won't go there right now, though. That's too personal still. Which brings me to the bigger issue that I want to run by you: the duel nature of reality. The being and non-being of life. And the Way. I want to ask you something. Do those souls centered in their non-being get pulled into false teachings because of their state of non-being consciousness, or inauthenticity if you will? Because that's what I feel happened to me. Is this why I was pulled into two false teachings?"

"Essentially, yes; but that's a loaded question, because one is never one or the other. Soul is always both being and non-being, and it chooses which path to follow. But there is a gravitational factor involved also, and that is what you are referring to. The law of attraction works to pull one where he has to go to learn his karmic lessons, and you were pulled into two false teachings for karmic reasons; that's the answer to your question."

"Okay, we're getting close to the answer I'm looking for. I want to know how much more I have to endure to rid myself of what Jesus called 'the worm' in Jung's *Red Book;* and by 'worm' I mean my vanity issue. How much more do I have to learn to rid myself of this insidious creature?"

"You're almost there, my good friend. You are much closer than you think, because becoming conscious of this creature has always been the biggest hurdle; but you are over the hurdle now, and the rest is simple housecleaning."

"I'd like to walk away gracefully from my spiritual community, but I don't know if that's possible. I have a heavy heart, and the only cure I can think of is to write my story and get it out of my system, and I don't think I'm going to be too kind in my story because I want to bring the community's hypocrisy to light."

"There is no disgrace in shining the light into dark corners. Shine your light and let the world be your judge."

153

"Okay, tell me your secret now. How do you always see the positive side of my life? You never ever focus on the negative. How do you do it?"

"With love and compassion. I've been trained to love everyone. I spent most of my life in the confessional listening to people's woes and sorrows, and I learned to love every single one of them. I've been well trained, my friend."

"You did give me a whole new perspective on confession, and I appreciate it very much. I have to share something with you, now that I think about it. Carl Jung made a comment that he did not get many Catholics for psychotherapy, and he attributed that to the confessional. He said that psychotherapy was a kind of secular confessional, and I think he was right; because you were a kind of psychotherapist to your penitents, were you not?"

"That and much more. I had to be father, mother, doctor, teacher, and God's holy representative for all my penitents. As I said, I was well trained. That's why I always see the positive side of life. I was taught by my penitents to see the positive side of life, because if I stressed the negative, which I did at the beginning, they always came back feeling worse; and then I made the connection and always accented the positive, regardless how bad it looked for them. And it worked, because God's energy seemed to flow much more freely that way."

"I'd like to cultivate that attitude."

"What's stopping you?"

"Me, I guess; what else? I'm always standing in my own way. I guess I have to learn to step aside and let myself be the person I want to be."

"That's the struggle. Being one's self free of one's personal impediments has always been the hardest part of the journey; but it's yours for the asking"

"I'm asking!"

"Love and compassion. Kindness and understanding. Forgiveness. These are your bywords. Live by them and you will remove the impediments that stand in your way. It is not as difficult as you may think, once you get started."

"Here's a question: Penny kissed me on the cheek and thanked me for writing *In the Shade of the Maple Tree*, because she said it helped her overcome many of her anxieties; will the average reader feel the same about this book?"

"This is the book's virtue. Yes, many readers will appreciate the wisdom that comes through, at your expense of course; but they will praise you for your courage to put yourself out there for everyone to see. I praise you for that too."

"I don't need praise. I need readers!"

"Readers will come when they are called; that is the law. After all, how did you find your way if not through the many books that you were called to read? Give yourself a chance; time will spare you of the indignity you feel."

"Penny just called me for my morning chores, so I have to sign off now. Maybe we can talk later; I'll see."

"Ciao for now, then..."

+

45. The Freshness of the Day

Saturday, June 6, 2015

"Good morning, Padre. I just posted another spiritual musing on my blog; it's called "The Same Old Question," (which is, for the record, "what is the purpose of my life?"), and I answered: to be who we are meant to be. But I don't know if this will have any effect or not on the readers of my blog, because people ask the question and then slide back into what Wordsworth called "the light of common day." Which brings me to the phrase that popped into my mind this morning, a phrase I thought I had read in one of Wordsworth's poems but couldn't find when I checked to look for it, a phrase that speaks to how I feel about life today, a feeling I would love to recapture, that special feeling that comes with *"the freshness of the day."* That's the phrase, then; but can I ever recapture the freshness of the day? That's what I'd like to talk about this morning, if you are up to suffering my pesky melancholy demon that has taken up residence in my mind this morning because I'm suffering from what I think could be the beginning of a tooth problem: I have a faint dull pain in one of my back teeth, and I hate going to the dentist as much as I hate going to doctors and funerals and weddings. So if you will bear with me, can we talk?"

"You do put a smile on my face, my friend. Of course we can talk. But before we do, let me share my feelings on the book In the Shade of the Maple Tree that Penny is reading while we are chatting; I also think like her that this book is very therapeutic, and that it will do the average reader a lot of good. And I understand why you would not place that high a value on it, because it is only a 'process' for you, as you explained to Penny; but it is a process that speaks to the problems of everyday life, just as Penny said. So just keep on sharing your thoughts this way; it is a genre all of its own and it has its merits. Penny just told you that this is her favorite read of all your books; and what does that tell you?"

"Strangely enough, I had reservations about giving it to her to read; and she had to keep insisting until I finally gave in. I didn't want to ask her about it as she read it, because I feared how it would affect her; the more she read, the more she liked it, and now she calls it her favorite book. Go figure? And now she's asking to read my book *The Summoning of Noman*, which I have also hesitated giving to her because it is so personal; but this morning I called up my file and went through it again, and then Penny and I found a picture from Bigstock Photos for the cover, a photo of an open book, gavel, and scales of justice to symbolize the summoning of Noman, and I'm going to give Penny the file today so she can edit and format it for publication. What do you think? Is my apprehension ill-founded?"

"It is a very personal book, one of your most personal; but again, it speaks to another dimension of life that needs to be out there, the concept of parallel lives that you are currently experiencing because this is the second time you have lived your life as Orest Stocco. So, no; you need not be apprehensive."

"Now, about how I feel about leaving my spiritual community and the New Age teaching of the Light and Sound of God that I lived for thirty-odd years, I still have some issues to work out. I know I have to write them out of my system, which I hope to do when I write my story 'The Funeral Service,' but I think I'd still like to discuss this a little more with you. I want to share a dream I had while I was writing *The Summoning of Noman*, because this dream speaks to my walking away from this spiritual teaching of the Light and Sound of God: I'm in a large hall and followers of this teaching are coming in to listen to the Spiritual Leader of this teaching. The followers sit down, and the Inner Master walks onto the stage. The Inner Master is the leader of this teaching. I'm standing on the stage behind the Inner Master watching. When everyone is sitting down they stare at the Inner Master full of expectation, but the Inner Master looks at them and then snaps his fingers and all of a sudden everyone in the audience wakes up from their hypnotic spell. That's the dream, and I believe it speaks to the spell they were under by this teaching; because the real Inner Master is their Higher Self, and their Higher Self will eventually snap his fingers and wake them up from their hypnotic spell. Wasn't that a wonderful dream, and several years before I walked away from this teaching?"

"As you said in The Summoning of Noman, 'dreams don't lie.' Yes, that was a wonderful dream. It foretold your departure from your

teaching. This is another reason why you should get The Summoning of Noman out there. Give it to Penny today so she can begin working on it."

"Life seems to be a series of waking up experiences, doesn't it? We go from one state of consciousness to another until we wake up to our true self, isn't that the way it seems to be? Because if this is the case, then all these different spiritual teachings are nothing but aids to waking us up from life—including the false teachings like the two that I studied; or is it three, because my Roman Catholic faith as I grew up is founded upon the lie that we only live one life that Jesus died on the cross to save for us. We live many lives, and we have to work out our own salvation, as St. Paul said in one of his letters; so what's all the fuss about, then? All of these teachings are nothing but aids to waking us up, that's all. I don't know what I'm trying to say, Padre. I think I'm still angry with myself for not waking up to the lie of my spiritual path, and I'm just venting to let the pressure out."

"Yes, you are; and it is good for you. You have the gift of writing to vent your emotions where most people don't and they suffer much more than you; so be thankful for your writing. It spares you a lot of grief."

"You know, Padre; I think I know what I've been trying to say to you for a long time now. I'm trying to say that all of this effort to wake up to life by committing to one teaching or another doesn't really matter, because it's going to happen anyway as we live our life. Life will wake us up eventually, be it through a teaching aid or not; so why bother? Am I being fair to the seeker?"

"No. Just ask yourself where you would be if you didn't become a seeker. You would be still back there, making a good living in your business; and you would not have achieved what you have achieved because you became a seeker. You are just angry for not waking up soon enough to the lie of your spiritual path, that's all; but it's time to get over it and get on with your life. You have many books to write yet, and your days are getting numbered. Don't fret just yet, but you have to start planning your time more efficiently. You have at least ten more books to write, so don't waste your time about what could have been or should have been. Could have been and should have been are just ways to ease your conscience, but you paid in full for what you received from life, and you have been rewarded; so no

more could have been and should have been. JUST DO. Make this your motto, and you will once again experience the freshness of the day because DOING always brings in fresh energy from the Creative Stream of Life. Okay, my friend?"

"You come in loud and clear, Padre. You always do, but I do have a stubborn streak that I don't think I'll ever get rid of. I wouldn't mind so much being stubborn, but my stubborn streak is stupid; and that annoys me. I guess that's why I had to write my book *Stupidity Is Not a Gift of God*. But thank you for reminding me. I have to ask you though before singing off: is my dull tooth ache symptomatic of an emotional or spiritual problem? By this I mean, what am I holding back that's causing this dull ache? I sense that I'm not in agreement with myself."

"You're right. You are not being true to your calling. You keep putting off your writing. Write your dull ache out of your system. Get back to your Gurdjieff book. That's where the problem started. It's the issue with your mother that you don't want to write about. Write it, and your ache will go away. I promise."

"I have been putting it off, haven't I? Okay, I'll get back to it once I get my day's obligations out of the way. I'm going into Midland to pick up my weekend papers, which I have to read because they give me ideas for my spiritual musings and keep me abreast of what Jesus called 'life and the living.' So, until we talk again, thank you for your patient understanding."

"You're welcome. Go about your business, and get back to your book. It needs your full attention. That's all I have to say."

"Enough said. *Ciao*, Padre…"

46. My Need for Knowledge

Sunday, June 7, 2015

"Good morning, Padre. I woke up a little more rested this morning. The dull ache in my tooth seems to be gone. I noticed last night when I ate some cold watermelon that the cold activated the pain in my tooth, but it gradually went away; and before we went to bed Penny and I took a spoonful of organic honey because of its many benefits, one being that it helps one to sleep better. I didn't' take the honey for my dull tooth ache, just to get some sleep. We've been taking it for about a week and a half now, and in all honesty both Penny and I think it's working; and I'll try anything to get a good night's sleep. But that's not why I'm initiating this talk today; I want to ask you something. Why do I have this craving for knowledge? Not just any knowledge, because I'm not interested in knowledge about everything; only that knowledge which will enlighten me on the human condition. I want to know about our life, about the human psyche, about the mystery of man. Why? This morning, for example, rather than get into writing my Gurdjieff book I went to my Amazon Wish List and checked out some books I'm thinking of ordering, and I checked out some books on Jung. I love the Look Inside feature that Amazon offers, so I can get to read what the book has to offer; and I often read the Introduction, Preface, and a chapter or two, sometimes everything they have to offer. This gives me a good idea whether to order the book or not. So, why do I have this need for knowledge about the nature of man and the human condition? Is it past-life related? Is it genetic, insomuch that I feel that I was born with what I humorously call an 'ignorance gene,' which I believe I inherited from my family tree, that southern Italian superstitious and non-literate peasantry? How close am I in this feeling?"

"You're right on all accounts, but it is very complex and difficult to explain because it goes back to why life exists in the first place. As you have surmised with your creative writing, life is here to expand the consciousness of God; and the need for God knowledge is

implanted in every soul. God knowledge is knowledge of the Whole, so soul needs to fill itself with knowledge to be more itself; this is the basic explanation for man's need for knowledge. God is all knowledge, and the need for knowledge is to soul what food is to the living organism, what water is to fish, and what air is to all living things; we need it to survive. Soul needs knowledge to survive, and depending upon a soul's karmic destiny it will seek out knowledge specific to its need to complete its destiny. You need knowledge about man and the human condition because you want to understand why you are and how to become whole and complete. Even though you have realized your wholeness, you still need knowledge—the essence of God, if you will—to grow more into yourself; and so you read and read and read. But you must realize that the essence of God comes through more directly when you engage what Jung called the 'transcendent function,' which simply means that you connect with the Creative Life Stream with your writing as the case may be. An artist would connect with his art, a musician with his music, and sculptor with his sculpting and one who loves his work will connect with the archetypal energy of his work. That's what drives man to become, their need for the essential energy of God that is the knowledge of what is. Your need for knowledge of man and the human condition is your need for what is; and I have told you time and again that DOING connects to what is. Does that answer your question?"

"Not quite. I'd like to clear something up, if I may. DOING, as you say, connects one with what is, or the Creative Life Stream—which is the essential energy of God, or the life force if you will—but if my need is so great, why do I procrastinate in DOING? Do you see where I'm going with this? The thirsty man does not snub his nose at a drink of water, nor does a hungry man turn his back on food; so why my obstinacy when I already know how to nourish my need for the essence of God? Why do I forsake myself?"

"Commitment requires effort, and effort requires energy, and you don't have the energy you used to have. You used to have inexhaustible amounts of energy, but your heart condition changed all of that, and you have lost steam. You are not the man you used to be, as no one is as they grow in years, especially if they grow with medical conditions. So you don't expend your energy like you used to. You unconsciously preserve your energy for simpler things, things

161

that don't require that much effort; because the more effort it requires, the more exhausted you feel. That's the simple answer. The more complete answer has to do with how tired you feel about your search. You have spent yourself finding yourself, and you would like to go on a long holiday; but because you cannot go on a long holiday, you do the next best thing: you do as little as possible. That's your answer."

"Okay, I see you are at your finest today, telling me what I need to know without mincing words, and I guess there's no need to pursue this any further. It all comes back to choice: what do I do with myself? Do I make the best of my situation, or do I just continue doing what I do until it's time to cross over? It seems that's the path I'm on, and I don't like myself for it."

"Then do something about it. It's not that difficult. Just shift direction a little. You'd be amazed what you can accomplish with the slightest shift in direction. A whole new trajectory opens up to you with each shift in direction. This is a law of physics. If you start to ride your bike or go for a walk each day, it will be a shift from not riding your bike or going for a walk, and this opens up a whole new trajectory which will take you in another direction. That's why I keep insisting that you write and write and write, because writing connects you with the essential energy of God, or life force if you prefer, and this energy is inherently self-lifting. All you have to do is connect every day with your creative center and then go for a walk or ride your stationary bike or your mountain bike and that will motivate you to do more, because the man who does always does more. And of course, the man who does not always does less. This is also a law of nature."

"Okay, I'm putting off writing about my relationship with my mother. I'm planning to write about *la fascino*. Did your mother believe in that?"

"Yes, certainly; most Italians do. But especially the southern Italians where poverty ruled the day. Superstition is paramount where there is ignorance, but because there is ignorance does not rule out the truth behind the superstition. You know that there is a great truth behind la fascino. That's why you want to write about it, and I'm glad you are; because this will tie in beautifully with the 'way of the sly man' that you lived by when you were deep into your search for

knowledge of the human condition. You had to know what it meant to draw energy from another, and la fascino was one way of doing it. Explain la fascino for your reader. For the record here, la fascino was the folk belief that the evil eye robbed one of their life force; and someone who knew how to avert the evil eye was considered gifted. Your mother knew how to do the prayer ritual that broke the curse of the evil eye. That's what you want to write about, so do it. Don't hesitate. It's this kind of hidden knowledge that will help to explain your path to your true self to your readers. La fascino was of great assistance to you, and you have an obligation to explain it. That, incidentally, is also a law; it is the Spiritual Law of Balance."

"When I google-translated the word *la fascino,* the English translation came out as 'charmed', which simply means that one is charmed, or 'cursed' as the case may be; and my mother had a prayer ritual that broke the curse of *la fascino,* and she taught this prayer ritual to me. It was passed on one Christmas Eve, as was the custom; but I was the only one in the family who wanted to know this."

"You're siblings did not have the need to know as you did. It was enough for them to have your mother say the ritual prayers for them. My mother did the same for me and my family. She was also blessed with the gift."

"But the irony is that because God is infinite so is knowledge, and my need for God knowledge would also be infinite, and this makes me hopelessly addictive because I will never get enough; do you see the irony?"

"You do make me smile. Yes, you are addicted to God just as I was and every seeker after truth. This is the human condition. As I like to say, it is what it is."

"And so it comes right back to this: my life, my choice?"

"Exactly. How do you want to live your life? DOING, my friend; that's the answer to your dilemma. Do what you are called to do."

"Well, I was called to talk with you this morning; and that's what I'm doing. I learned something from you this morning, too. The man who does will do more, and the man who does less will do less still; that's the knowledge I got from you this morning, which is the same knowledge that Jesus gave to the world in his saying about dying to one's life to gain one's life. It's all about the law of attraction, isn't it? That's the knowledge of the human condition that has spawned the whole get rich industry in the self-help movement, sparked by a book called *The Secret* if I'm not mistaken. It's all so boring, to tell you the truth. That's why I wrote my musing 'The Same Old Questions that I posted on my blog yesterday.' We know the answer, but it's the application that gets to us; some of us are more industrious than others, so we can't blame anyone for our condition, can we? I'd better stop whining then and get on with my life and make the tough choices. That's where I'm at today."

"That's where everyone is at. You simply recognize it, that's all. But in that, you have to face yourself long enough to become aware that you write the script of your own life; most people won't stand still long enough for that. They drive themselves unconsciously so they don't have to face the reality of their life; that's why life has to do the work for them and bring them to a standstill with a traumatic life experience. That always make people stop and think."

"Yes, I know; life is inherently self-correcting, isn't it?"

"Absolutely. What we won't do ourselves, life forces us to do eventually because life is the benevolent energy of God that is inherently self-lifting, and when life gives us a traumatic experience it's for our own good. This is the mystery behind Christ's comment about the beauty of suffering in Jung's Red Book. Christ knew the glory of suffering, and he shared that with the world. That was my gift, and I am honored to share it with the world also. Suffering is a mystery still, though; but you can help take the mystery out with your understanding. You have the knowledge, and you have been called to share it in your writing. Just do it, my friend."

"I know, I know; but I am a procrastinator. That's not an excuse; that's my condition. And the only way to change that is to make a shift in my trajectory, right? All I have to do is make one little shift, because that opens the door to a whole new archetypal pattern which will grant me access to more uplifting energy? Isn't that how it works, according to the metaphysics of this knowledge?"

"Yes. Now let's call it a day so you can get on with your writing. Just start and see where it takes you. Have a joyful day, my friend."

"*Ciao,* Padre; and thank you…"

47. Let God and Let Be

Monday, June 8, 2015

"Good morning, Padre. Penny and I proofed *In the Shade of the Maple Tree* yesterday and now Penny can publish it on Lulu; but I want to tell you this morning that on our drive to the Blue Sky Restaurant for breakfast yesterday morning the book came up in conversation and I ended up calling it my 'incidental book.' I said this because I don't even consider it a book. I just sat down and talked with you, and out of our talks came the first volume of our dialogues which Penny has now called her favorite book; so I said to her that it was a book that just happened, like someone going to work one day and something happened along the way, one of those experiences that can change one's life. One has an incident, as it were; this is why I called *In the Shade of the Maple Tree* my incidental book. There's something else I want to share with you. Penny found the book very comforting, and she said that she didn't even question your validity until I brought it up in our talks. Only when I suggested that you are a product of active imagination did she think about you not being a real entity (I was going to say person, but you are on the Other Side in spirit); that's how credibly you come across in our talks. So, I guess what you have to say to me might just be independent of my own mid. But as you said, what does it matter? As long as it's working, it serves its purpose. Now I'm talking just for the sake of talking. I don't have anything specific I want to talk about; I just feel listless. I did have a topic I wanted to talk with you about, but I deleted my notes this morning because I didn't want to go there just yet. Maybe I do, though. It has to do with spiritual paths and the ontology of our being. Here's the question, then: are the false spiritual paths in life inevitable given the non-being dimension of our ontology? In effect, are false spiritual paths necessary to assist soul on its way to non-dual reality, if you know what I mean? Can we begin there?"

"You are very listless, my friend; but that's okay. You are going through a transformation which you are not conscious of. This

is because you have broken away from your spiritual path and are now on your own. You are experiencing the freedom of your independence, and you are wandering about in spirit; but you will find your footing within a few weeks. It takes time to let go of your emotional attachment to your spiritual path; but it was necessary. You would not have taken the next step in your journey. Now you have, which is why you can ask me this kind of question. Yes, you are right; false spiritual paths are a way of life, and they are also part of the Divine Plan of God. Soul has to work its way through its own non-being, and false spiritual paths speed up the process just as all true spiritual paths speed up the process; they are two sides of the same coin. And because you are going to ask, the same coin is the Way."

"You mean a false path is the shadow side of the Way?"

"Yes."

"But these false paths make themselves out to be genuine. At least, the spiritual path that I have just left does. Is it a genuine spiritual path?"

"No. It's a false path. Its premise is false. It purports its Spiritual Leader to have God consciousness, a God-realized man; but that's fabricated."

"You're being very specific. Why?"

"You asked me."

"Yes, I did. I didn't want to know before, but I do now. This is what I've been thinking about lately. If the Spiritual Leader of this teaching is not what he says he is, then he's perpetrating a lie upon his spiritual community; but what does this tell me? What am I to make of this? I bought into this lie for over thirty years and only now do I find out? Am I a fool, or what?"

"I bought into my Roman Catholic faith all of my life, but much of it was fabricated from the truth of our Lord's teaching; does that make me a fool too? It's all a question of need. What soul needs for its journey to wholeness, life will provide. It is the Law of Life."

"You didn't answer my question. Was I a fool?"

"No less than I was."

"Alright, I know the answer: we were both fools for God!"

"Yes, my friend; we were both fools for God, and the laugh is on the deceivers, not us. We are genuine in our belief, and that's all that matters. How the world deals with deceivers is not our concern.

Life has its ways, and as the Preacher said in the Book of Ecclesiastes, 'God shall bring every work into judgement.' Don't worry your head over this. You are free of its unconscious hold on you, and you have moved on. Let go and let be."

"I like that, 'let go and let be.' I don't think I ever heard that expression before, but it fits perfectly here; doesn't it?"

"Yes, because it is perfectly non-judgemental."

"I wasn't going to pursue the subject—pardon me, Padre; but I have to for just a while longer. Is the Spiritual Leader of this teaching aware of his own lie? Does he know that he is not what he purports to be?"

"Now we're getting into deep water. A person can become what they believe, and he has gone as far as he can in his belief. His job is to keep his followers believing that he is what he says he is, and as long as they believe they will grow in their path; this is the merciful nature of the Law of Life. God does not abandon any soul, whatever path it's on. The path that a soul is on is the path it needs for its growth. You needed this path and it served you well. Can't you just leave it at that?"

"You know I can't. I'm a writer with a need to know. I need to know what the hell is going on—pardon my language, Padre. I apologize. No need to get emotional. I just need to know so I can find closure."

"You're intentions are honorable, but you do upset yourself unnecessarily. You will get the knowledge you need in the fullness of time."

"Alright, I'll leave it for now; but I want it on record that I'm not happy. I think this whole thing stinks to high heaven, and what bothers me so much about it is that all these years I thought the world was stupid for what it believed about this teaching, but in its ignorance the world was right and I was the fool. That's an irony too heavy to bear. Do you see why I feel as I do? I have to suffer my humiliation in private, and I want to hate myself for being such a gullible fool. I'm sorry, Padre; but I can't help myself."

"If I may confess my own feelings about this whole thing, let me tell you that I went through something like you are going through when I became aware of the fabricated truth of my faith, and I had to

bear that alone too. It's not a nice place to be, but this is the price one pays for truth. What do you think the path to truth is all about anyway, if not a walk through the lies of life?"

"So you're saying that this is as necessary as the seasons?"

"Very well put. The seasons are necessary, and winter is followed by spring and summer. You have journeyed through the winter of your discontent, and now you are into the joy of spring and summer, the growing seasons; and then comes the harvest of the fall to make you ready for another winter of discontent, if that winter should come at all. It may not for you, my friend; it all depends upon what you harvest in the fall of your life."

"I love the analogy. So our karma determines what kind of winter we're going to have, is that it?"

"Essentially, yes. We reap what we sow."

"I don't know what else I can say. I think you have given me what I need to get on with my day. I do have one more dreadful thought that I have to run by you, if I may. I've been plagued with the dreaded feeling that my imagination for my own becoming may have run out of steam, and I have difficulty imagining myself being what I want to be, more fit and healthy, and more disciplined and determined. I've run out of imagination, and this scares me!"

"Go to your Wordsworth. Read his Resolution and Independence. Think of the Leech Gatherer on the lonely moor. You have much to be grateful for; now you have to make yourself aware of what you have, and build on that. Don't worry about what you don't have. Wordsworth lost his melancholy after he met the Leech Gatherer on the lonely moor. Imagine yourself on the lonely moor and meet your own Leech Gatherer. Do the exercise. It will do you good."

"Sorry, Padre; I have to take out the garbage and blue boxes, and then have morning coffee with Penny. We'll talk later...

"I'll be here..."

Later...

"I'm back, and with a new theme to discuss with you. I've got to write a new spiritual musing for my blog because I posted my last one the other day, and while Penny and I were talking about the movie we watched online last night, *The Angriest Man in Brooklyn*, starring Robin Williams, Penny said to me, 'I smell a musing coming on,' and she was right; I felt my Muse touch me on the shoulder and whisper into my ear, 'Do a musing on anger.' But before I do, I'd like to run the theme by you, because from all the books that I read on your life I know that you had to stare down your demon anger that was engendered (if that's the right word) by all your detractors. I know your answer already, because you revealed this to me already; but I want to know if you did anything more than pray for your 'enemies.'"

"I did pray and pray and pray, because they hurt me deeply for something that I did not do. I was what I was, and it hurt me deeply to be called a fake and deceiver. That's the worst thing I could have been accused of being. I was true to my Lord and Savior, and I never wavered. But as to anger, I had to bite my tongue so often that I must have set a new world record. I don't know what to tell you, but I can inform you that anger is a nasty demon."

"I went through a long period of anger that I could not understand, and which I believe was brought on by my feelings for my spiritual community, probably started around the time that I cracked a tooth at one of our spiritual functions which I wrote about in my musings; but it lasted a long time, and it finally kept me away from our spiritual community functions. So I know anger very well. And I experienced anger many times before, but not as deeply; so I think I'm well qualified to write a spiritual musing on anger. I just want to discuss this emotion with you before I do, though; if you don't mind."

"Not at all. Anger is as common to man as rain is to the weather. It comes and it goes, but when it comes life can drown one in the emotion, and that can be devastating for one and their close ones. Anger comes from failed efforts, from unrealized dreams and expectations, and especially from the reality of one's own shortcomings. It's hard to accept the truth about one's life, and rather than acknowledge the truth one points the finger; and that's the demon's victory, because the fault lies in oneself and not the other. That's what spared me from being possessed by my demon anger whenever I was falsely branded. I knew the truth about myself, and I sought refuge in my Lord Jesus. But what happens to a person who

has neither the courage to acknowledge their own shortcomings nor a place of refuge from their demon anger? That's what happened to the Robin William's character Henry Altmann in the movie The Angriest Man in Brooklyn; he was angry at life but had no refuge. His refuge turned out to be his family, which redeemed him in the end; so the theme of your musing should be about truth and self-deception, and a place of refuge from one's demon anger."

"Wonderful. I'll give it to my Muse. Anything else you'd like to say before I turn it over to my creative unconscious?"

"Trust in the creative process. Start it and see where it takes you."

"I will, as soon as we sign off. *Ciao* for now, then."

"One piece of advice, if I may. Don't be afraid to be personal, because the personal speaks to the universal. Okay, ciao my friend..."

48. On the Front Deck

Tuesday, June 9, 2015

"Padre, I'm sitting here on our front deck initiating this dialogue with pen and paper and not on my computer as I normally do because I want to be outside, and the gentle rain makes this dialogue a little more natural, a little more real, like the talk we had in the shade of the maple tree that initiated this exercise in active imagination; so if you would allow me to speak freely, I have a few things I have to run by you because our second volume of dialogues (last night Penny put out the Kindle version of *In the Shade of the Maple Tree*, the first volume of our talks together) has grown enough to bring to closure with today's dialogue and one more, which will bring it to 49 talks, a nice number for *The Man of God Walks Alone*. So, I welcome you to our covered front deck where we can take in the fresh air with the gentle rain falling. I don't know what I'm going to say, but I feel I'm bursting; so much pressure and anxiety that my teeth are hurting, and I'm not kidding."

"Good morning, my friend. It is a lovely day with the gentle rain falling, a reminder of the days I sat in the garden under a tree as the rain soaked our garden. Those were wonderful days for me in San Giovanni. Now, your teeth are hurting because you are anxious for putting off your household obligations. You do that all the time and try to justify your failure to live up to your end of the family responsibilities by hiding behind your writing; but you cannot fool yourself, and your anxiety works its way into your body through the tension in your jaw that makes your teeth hurt."

"I agree, and I hate myself for being such a coward. But I can hear time's winged chariot drawing near and I want to leave the best of me behind in my writing and not in my household chores. I know that's not fair to Penny, and myself even, but writing is more important now than it ever was, especially now that I am no longer driven by the vanity of my need to be published and acknowledged; I'm driven instead by my creative daemon that has been slain of the vanity that made my life unbearable, and I love what comes through in my writing now. So if I may, let me ask you some questions as they come to me. The first being, why do I feel no more empathy for the plight of the human condition?"

"As you said to Penny this morning, your objectivity has freed you of your emotional attachment to the world situation, and man's suffering no longer affects you as it used to. But you still care, only from a detached perspective. This is as it should be, because now you have more clarity."

"Padre, I want to cry. I want to bawl my head off. I want to just sit and cry and cry and cry. I want to quit my life, but I cannot for Penny's sake, and my heart is heavy with sacred knowledge that no one cares to hear. It pains me see how the world passes by, everyone involved in this and that without a thought about the big WHY. It makes me cry. What am I to do?"

"Write. Lose yourself in your writing. When your conscience can no longer suffer the guilt of your procrastination do what you have to do and you will then write without suffering the guilt of omission. Just do what you have to do to bring this current book to closure, and then you can get on with another book of dialogues which will be even better than the first two; I promise you."

"Why do I feel like crying?"

"Your heart is still heavy from leaving your spiritual path. You have walked away and it's been a long, long journey; and you feel sorry for all the time you think you wasted on this path. But you needed that experience to grow in your true self. It was necessary, and you have no need to be regretful. Walk away and let your experience with this teaching seep into the story that you are going to write on your relationship with your spiritual community; it will be a story to remember. I can promise you will find that writing this story will be one of your most rewarding creative efforts."

"I hope so…"

Later in the day…

"It's 2:40 in the afternoon. I've put on dinner and gone for a short walk. I made a sauce. I fried some diced onions, one clove of garlic chopped, one red pepper diced, several stalks of celery cut into small pieces, and two carrots diced, and then I added several tablespoons of olive oil, and I let them sauté for five or ten minutes; and then I added four Italian sausages cut into one inch pieces, and chicken giblets that I had boiled twice, rinsing the water the second time (which I learned from my mother), and I added salt, pepper, and dried basil and let everything cook for ten minutes before adding a can of tomato paste and a can of whole tomatoes, which I cut into pieces before putting them into my pot, and I let the sauce simmer for several hours. I just checked the pot now, and the sauce tastes wonderful; and when Penny comes home from work I'll add the orecchiette into the sauce. Orecchiette is an ear-shaped pasta, from the Italian word 'orrechi,' which means ear. So I'm free to continue our talk because I have to get something clear. I don't know where I am today, and haven't known where I've been for several days now; and I don't like this feeling. It's like I've been marooned on a distant shore ever since Penny and I walked away from our spiritual path once I got confirmation online that the founder of this teaching fabricated the whole thing for reasons which still baffle me, and I don't know where I am Padre; can you tell me? I don't feel lost, as such; just marooned on an island, or is it a whole new continent that I'm not aware of? What's going on with me?"

"I wish I could be invited for dinner. I can smell your sauce, and it brings back memories of my mother. How I loved her simple cooking! I'm very proud of you, my friend. You do your mother proud. Now, let's get serious for a moment and discuss your situation. You are not lost. How can you be? You spent your whole life looking for the ground of your being, and you stand solidly on who you have become. You are you, and the continent of your being is your life; so don't fret about not knowing where you are. You don't feel lost, just marooned as you say; but let's look up this word marooned, shall we?"

"I'll just skip over to my sidebar dictionary....Okay, I've got it. Marooned means, 'leave stranded or isolated with little hope of rescue.' Is that how I feel? Do I feel that my spiritual path has stranded me, or have I stranded it? I walked away from it, didn't I? Who stranded who, is that what you want me to know? What is it you want to tell me, Padre?"

"Your spiritual path stranded you with its false teaching, that's why you feel as you do. You became conscious of the fabricated mythology of this teaching and you walked away because you felt it had left you stranded on a path that had no real ground under its feet. That's why you want to cry and cry and cry. You invested a lot of time and energy into this teaching, and you paid handsomely for it; and now here you are—"

"I have to go, Padre; Penny just pulled into the yard. Please bear with me; we'll talk later…"

Later…

"This is an interrupted dialogue. Sorry for all the bother, but I do feel like something is happening. Back to the issue, my spiritual path stranded me with little hope of rescue because there's no chance I'd never go back knowing what I know now. It's a false path, but I guess it's necessary for those that need it; apparently, like I did. So am I a fool or what?"

"We've gone over this. No, you are not a fool; just a man who dared to risk going where he was called. If you recall, that path came right to your house; and if that isn't the call of Soul, what is?"

"So a person can be called to a false path, then?"

"You did. Not once, but twice."

"Right, the other was that offshoot Christian solar cult teaching. I wish I could write that story. It's been a long time since I thought about "The Sunworshipper," but that's the teaching that did irreparable damage to my eyesight."

"Not you alone, many followers of that teaching damaged their eyes; but the lessons were learned and that's how life works."

"Okay, back to where I started this dialogue. I want to bring closure to *The Man of God Walks Alone,* and I have one more dialogue with you after this one; but I'm not quite comfortable with what I wanted to say today. It's like I've avoided what I wanted to say, and I'm going to rest a while and read over what we talked about and take it from there; so please bear with me."

"We'll talk soon. Ciao, my friend…"

49. The Emperor Has No Clothes

Thursday, June 11, 2015

"Well, Padre; how am I to feel now that I know that the emperor has no clothes? Did it have to take more than thirty years for me to see that the founder of the spiritual path that I embraced had woven an invisible garment for his leadership of the spiritual path he fabricated out of ancient teachings that he borrowed, stole, and plagiarized from other sources? Why did it take me so long to snap out of the hypnotic spell this teaching had upon me? But before you answer me, let me tell you that while I was working on my book *The Summoning of Noman* I had a dream about the Inner Master of this spiritual path who snapped his fingers and woke up all his followers from the hypnotic spell they were under, and I witnessed the whole thing from the stage where I was standing behind the Inner Master. Now, was the Inner Master, who was in the image of the spiritual leader of this path, *my* Inner Master and true teacher? Was this an *actual awakening* of the spiritual community that I have walked away from? What is going on, Padre? Was my unconscious foreshadowing my departure to make my experience of leaving my spiritual community less traumatic? Because it still leaves me with a heavy heart."

"Better a heavy heart than a traumatized mind. You were prepared by your Higher Self, or Divine Spirit if you will that came to you in your dream as the Inner Master of your spiritual teaching. You are correct in your understanding that the emperor has no clothes, and those who continue to follow this teaching do not want to know the truth. The vast majority don't know about the invisible garment that the spiritual leader of this community wears, and refuse to even entertain the idea that they are on a false path; and those that do look into it and stay have refused to admit to themselves that they have been fooled. But those that walk away have to come to terms with the teaching, as you are doing now. It has taken you a long time to admit to yourself that the emperor has no clothes, but from here on in it will

be easier for you to accept that the world is not what it seems. You are right to believe that false paths are necessary because it is all part of the enantiodromiac process of life, but this is too much for most people to understand. In time they will, and it is very good of you to bare your soul because this will embolden the less courageous. I understand this will be the final dialogue for this volume. Is there anything else that you would like to discuss with me before we bring closure?"

"I'm at a loss. I've grown weary of my journey through the lies and deceit of humanity, and I'd like to lie down and rest my weary soul. But you know what, Padre? What I'm coming to see is that it doesn't matter how the world unfolds, it only matters how I feel about myself; and I did my best to live an honest and decent life. I paid a heavy price to find my authentic self, and that's what my writing is all about; a journey through my own vanity to humility. So I have to thank you once again for my spiritual healing, because had I not written *Healing with Padre Pio* I'd still see the emperor wearing a beautiful garment of invisible clothes woven by a clever deceiver. Don't you think so?"

"No. You would have left eventually, but not with the grace that you did now. It would have been traumatic. Your spiritual musing 'The Parable of the Packages' says it all, in the most graceful way possible. It lets the teaching off the hook in one way because you placed it within a context that is acceptable, but you did reveal the emperor's invisible garment."

"I hate to bring closure to *The Man of God Walks Alone* with this talk, because it has me kneeling in the confessional beating my chest with '*Mea culpa.*' Being the Holy Father Confessor in San Giovanni de Rotondo, how do you respond to how I feel?"

"If this were then and you came to me for a confession for being taken in by a false spiritual teaching I would feel your pain first, which I always did when I heard my penitent's sins, and then I would bless you in the name of our Lord Jesus, the true teacher of salvation. I would give you the rosary to say two or three times every day for a month, and tell you to get back on the straight and narrow with the teachings of Jesus. That would be then. Today, where I am now in my consciousness of all knowing and seeing, I would say to you: you have received the lessons you were meant to learn to cleanse

your ego of the vanity that kept you from growing into the person you were meant to be, and having learned your lessons like your hero Carl Gustav Jung did, shake the dust off your feet and move on with your life in your enlightened understanding of life's deceitful ways. Write your story about your experience with this teaching to consolidate the reality of this deception into literary form, and this will be part of your legacy to literature. What else is there to say?"

"I've done a lot of research lately, listening to interviews on Conscious TV online, and I've been exposed to the 'non-dual' consciousness of many people, and I'm left wondering: are these people trapped in the non-reality of their own non-being, if I may express it this way? Actually, how else can I express the non-being of our own enantiodromiac nature?"

"That's the irony, isn't it? When they think they've arrived, the truth is that they are only half way there. The reality of one's true self is that it is both being and non-being and neither; it is Soul. You experienced the blending of the two selves into one; that is your journey, your story, and your truth which you wrote about in what will one day become a classic. I mean your book The Pearl of Great Price. You see the difference, and that is what you continue to write about. Trust your own experiences to guide your life. They have served you well before, and they will serve you well in the future. With respect to your spiritual community, you are now free of its unconscious hold upon you; and you are now free to speak your mind on the subject, if you so choose."

"The irony is that you knew about this spiritual teaching when I was writing *Healing with Padre Pio*, but you never once let on."

"It wasn't for you to know. How else could you have written that book, given that you believed in your spiritual teaching so firmly?"

"What about when I invited other Spiritual Masters to attend my spiritual healing sessions?"

"The genuine Masters that you invited came. Pythagoras came, and so did Master Zadok. The Spiritual Masters of your community were shadows, and I need not say more."

"Were they made of the consciousness of non-being?"

"That's a very good way of describing them. They were non-being masters that purported to be the real thing; they were Shadow

177

Masters. This is what Hans Christian Anderson meant by his fairy tale of the Emperor's New Clothes."

"Shadow Masters? Wow. Please elaborate."

"Shadow Masters manifest for those that have a desperate need to believe, and they do serve a purpose to satisfy this need; but they are only as real as one's need to believe, and as one grows through life experience and learns to walk on their own two feet Shadow Masters lose their power and disappear."

"Like me. I was so taken by Gurdjieff and his search for Spiritual Masters that I needed to believe, and I found one in the founder of the New Age spiritual teaching that I attracted into my life when I felt I had outgrown Gurdjieff's teaching. It was my need to believe in Spiritual Masters that attracted this teaching with its fraudulent mythology into my life, wasn't it?"

"Yes. But don't berate yourself. Soul needs what it needs, and all paths serve their purpose on soul's journey to wholeness. This teaching opened you up to spiritual concepts that expanded your awareness, which you needed to grow into the person you were meant to be; but once it served its purpose, you began to pull away. And when you were nudged to go for a spiritual healing with the psychic medium you saw an opportunity for a novel, and writing Healing with Padre Pio gave you the courage you needed to step back from your spiritual community; and the further you stepped back, the more clearly you saw through your community and the teaching until you saw that the emperor had no clothes."

"Padre, I feel like a limp rag. I need an infusion of inspiration so I can do what I've been called to do and write my stories; may I implore upon you to infuse me with inspiration to get me started? I have to move on from this teaching that took up so much of my time and energy, and I can't think of a better way than to bring everything that I have learned about life and the secret way into one simple perspective in the act of daily living. If there's one message that all of my writing could be reduced to, it would be that the simple act of daily living is the gateway to the kingdom of heaven that all of these spiritual paths and esoteric teachings promise; and that's the irony, isn't it?"

"How it warms my heart to hear you say that. After years of listening to my penitents, the secret way finally revealed itself to me in

the simple lives of the people who sought salvation from their sins. It dawned on me that without their sins there would be no road to salvation, and that's when I realized that life was the way God intended for every soul to grow. Life is the secret way, the one and only way to grow in love and understanding; all other ways are systems designed to speed up the process, and whether they are false or true teachings does not matter because life is a process of being and becoming. We cannot find truth without becoming aware of lies, and we have to walk through the lies of life to see the truth. I used to rant at the lies and hypocrisy of the world, but when I crossed over to this side I became aware of the dual nature of the self and saw that one was necessary for the other. We cannot have truth without lies, and we cannot have lies without truth; and we must walk a fine line as we work our way through the world. This is the journey of the self that every soul is on, and your journey has brought you through the biggest lie of your life which you lived for over thirty years; but you came out of this teaching with a knowledge and understanding that you would not have learned anywhere else, and you have grown to appreciate that there are many emperors in the world with invisible clothing. This was the lesson you were meant to learn, and now you can move on to where you have always wanted to be with those who value and honor truth as much as you do. Like attracts like, and you are no longer inhibited by the shadow of your spiritual community; so you will find a different sort of person gravitating into your life. I promise you."

"Sorry; I'm not hanging my hat on that. I'll continue to do what I do best and hope it happens, but I won't waste my time on reveries of meeting people who have transcended their being and non-being. If they come into my life, fine; and if not, that's fine too. On that note, Padre; we can call it a day."

"I've enjoyed our talks, my good friend; and I look forward to the third volume of our dialogues in active imagination. Ciao for now."

"*Ciao*, Padre…"

About the Author

Orest Stocco was born in Calabria, Italy. He emmigrated to Canada and studied philosophy at university. A student of Gurdjieff's teaching for many years, his passion for writing inspired such works as *The Summoning of Noman* and *The Pearl of Great Price.* He lives in Georgian Bay, Ontario with his life mate Penny Lynn Cates. His personal dictum is: Life is an individual journey.
Visit him at: http://ostocco.wix.com/ostocco
Spiritual Musings Blog:
http://www.spiritualmusingsbyoreststocco.blogspot.com

ME AND MY SISPHYEAN ROCK

www.ingramcontent.com/pod-product-compliance
Lightning Source LLC
LaVergne TN
LVHW091254080426
835510LV00007B/253